Modern Upholstering Methods
Second Edition

Modern Upholstering Methods
Second Edition

WILLIAM F. TIERNEY, Ed.D.
Retired Associate Professor, University of Maryland, College Park

American Literary Press, Inc.
Five Star Special Edition
Baltimore, Maryland

Modern Upholstering Methods
Second Edition

Library of Congress
Cataloging in Publication Data
ISBN 1-56167-315-3

Library of Congress Card Catalog Number:
96-084891

Published by

American Literary Press, Inc.
Five Star Special Edition
8019 Belair Road, Suite 10
Baltimore, Maryland 21236

Manufactured in the United States of America

Foreword

The art of upholstering provides an activity that is interesting, educational, and most useful to high school and college students, yet equally appealing to adults. Almost every home has at least one piece of upholstered furniture that is in need of reconditioning. Another amazing thing about upholstery is the success that a beginner can achieve if he is taught the fundamental "tricks of the trade."

The purpose of this book is to present answers to some of the problems encountered by beginners in upholstering, The beginning student or do-it-yourself enthusiast should first review the entire book and then study each section carefully as he progresses from one stage of his upholstery work to the next.

This book may serve as a useful text or reference for units on upholstery for industrial arts and home economics classes in the secondary schools and colleges. Many girls and women are able to perform upholstery work as well as, if not better than, some boys and men. Adult classes and do-it-yourself craftsmen will find this book especially helpful.

Emphasis is placed upon the situations which usually give the beginner the most difficulty. Such problems as computing the amount of material, laying out the fabric for cutting, attaching the fabric without wrinkles, sewing welting, making cushions, blind tacking, and attaching panels are thoroughly covered as well as fundamental operations dealing with frame construction and repair, attaching webbing, sewing and tying springs, positioning and anchoring stuffing materials, and the fabrication and use of foam rubber.

The various tools, as well as the techniques of using them, are explained from the standpoint of both the individual craftsman and mass production methods. The characteristics of various materials used in the furniture industry are discussed, and the best types are recommended for various conditions. Information is also included to give a picture of the upholstered furniture industry in general. Sources of supplies and their industrial manufacturing techniques are included.

Acknowledgments

The author wishes to express his deep appreciation to Dr. R. Lee Hornbake, Vice-President in charge of Academic Affairs, University of Maryland, for his inspiration and encouragement early in the preparation of this book. When he was head of our Industrial Education Department, he encouraged the writer to produce some upholstery articles for publication in a magazine. These became so voluminous that it was decided instead to develop a textbook on the subject. The author is further indebted to Dr. Donald Maley, present head of our Industrial Education Department for his continued interest and encouragement in relation to this textbook.

The writer also wishes to express his sincere appreciation to the students of his upholstery and woodworking courses who have contributed many ideas in regard to learning the art of upholstery and frame construction. The author is particularly indebted to those students who assisted in the production of photographs. Mr. Robert D. Herzog took and printed the industrial photographs at the Berkeley Upholstering Company in Martinsburg, West Virginia, through the courtesy of the proprietors, Mr. Sol Cohen and Mr. Robert Elins. Mr. Jerome Silverman took, developed, and printed many of the photographs showing work in progress in the author's classes. Mr. Lawrence Campbell and Mr. James H. Waddell also contributed some photographic work. Thanks are extended to Mr. Alan Brown for his line drawing of a trestle. Special recognition and gratitude is also extended to Kathleen E. Patrick (Mrs. James S. MacKenzie, Jr.) and Deborah A. Savage (Mrs. Jay Edwin Ricks) for permission to use pictures of themselves taken during the upholstery courses.

The author is further indebted to Carl S. Schramm, a departmental colleague, for assistance in taking and producing photographs of furniture, foam rubber products, and the fabrication of foam rubber at the University of Maryland and the following industries and businesses: American Forest Division of The American Excelsior Corporation, Baltimore, Maryland, fabricators of B. F. Goodrich products, courtesy of Paul E. Koehneke and John J. Corrigan; Northwest Supply Company, Washington, D.C., courtesy of Everett H. Johnson; and Julius Lansburgh Furniture Company, Hyattsville, Maryland, courtesy of Eric Smith.

The author is also indebted to his wife, Margaret, for her encouragement and assistance in typing early drafts of the manuscript; to his daughter, Margaret Elizabeth, for her persistent prodding, the typing of the final draft, and mounting of most of the illustrations; and to his young son for cooperation and patience shown in not disturbing materials for the manuscript.

Gratitude is also expressed to the following furniture manufacturers and upholsterers, tool and equipment manufacturers, and the Metropolitan Museum of Art either for their cooperation in providing illustrations or for permitting visits to and pictures to be taken in their establishments.

American Forrest Division, The American Excelsior Corp., Baltimore, Maryland
American Furniture Company, Batesville, Indiana
Armour and Company, Chicago, Illinois
Berkeley Upholstering Company, Martinsburg, West Virginia
Dunlop Tire and Rubber Corporation, Buffalo, New York
The Firestone Tire and Rubber Company, New York, New York
The B. F. Goodrich Sponge Products Division, Shelton, Connecticut
The Goodyear Tire and Rubber Company, Akron, Ohio
Heritage Furniture, Inc., High Point, North Carolina
Hickory Chair Manufacturing Company, Hickory, North Carolina
Kittinger Company, Inc., Buffalo, New York
Kroehler Manufacturing Company, Naperville, Illinois
Julius Lansburgh Furniture Company, Hyattsville, Maryland
Lochner Manufacturing Company, Fort Wayne, Indiana
Loyal Metal Products Company, Bronx, New York
Lumite Division, Chicopee Mills, Inc., New York, New York
The Mastland Duraleather Company, Philadelphia, Pennsylvania
The Metropolitan Museum of Art, New York, New York
George W. Mount, Greenfield, Massachusetts
Natural Rubber Bureau, Washington, District of Columbia
Northwest Supply Company, Washington, D.C.
C. S. Osborne and Company, Harrison, New Jersey
Reese's Antique Shop, Charlotte, North Carolina
The Singer Sewing Machine Company, New York, New York
Stanley Tools, New Britain, Connecticut
Union Brothers Furniture Company, Baltimore, Maryland
United States Rubber Company, New York, New York
The Upholstery Supply Company, Milwaukee, Wisconsin
Victorian Furniture Corporation, Montgomery, Alabama
J. Wiss and Sons Company, Newark, New Jersey

William F. Tierney

To
My wife Marg, daughter Peggy
and son Billy

Table of Contents

Glossary of Upholstering Terms

The purpose of this section is to acquaint the beginner with some of the more common terms used in upholstery. The list may supplement or serve as a guide for a demonstration in which the materials and tools are shown and explained to the student. This demonstration may well be the introductory or initial demonstration of the course.

Bridled edge — a built-up edge to keep stuffing from working away from the edge of the pad; formerly made entirely by hand; today formed rolled edging is usually used.

Burlap — cloth woven from jute yarn.

Cambric — cotton fabric, usually black, used as a dust cover for furniture bottoms.

Coconut fiber — outer husk of coconut used; less resilient than palm fiber.

Cotton felt — cotton linters spun into sheets and used as a pad over coarse stuffings and between temporary and final covers.

Cushion springs — a special seat spring knotted at both ends.

Down — feathers from young birds; undercoating of old birds such as ducks and geese.

Foam rubber — rubber with air bubbles in it; can be purchased in slab form for use as a stuffing material; expensive but very durable; used in molded form as cushion units.

Excelsior — made from basswood or poplar; not very resilient; used as a foundation in cheaper furniture.

Gimp — a fancy braid used to cover the edges of the cover where it meets the show wood and to conceal objectionable seams.

Gimp tacks — tacks that have a small round head; used for work where the head of the tack must show.

Hair — curled hair of horses, cattle, or hogs; used as a stuffing.

Kapok — silky fiber from seed pods of silk, cotton, or kapok tree; soft and fluffy; used in cushions and pillows.

Moss — a plant found in the Southern States; dried and shredded; forms a resilient stuffing material which does not attract moths.

Muslin — material used for temporary covers and as a general utility fabric.

Pad — a base on which stuffing is placed and then the whole is covered with a suitable textile, leather, or plastic.

Palm fiber — shredded leaves of palm tree; replacing tow as a good foundation.

Pillow springs — springs that are used for backs and arms; made of small gauge wire.

Regulator — needle-like device to even out irregularities in stuffing and to assist in shaping edges.

Ripping tool — a chisel-like tool used to strip old frames.

Rubberized hair — hair processed with rubber; strong, but more expensive than other hairs.

Skewer — a small wire device to fasten covers temporarily in place while being worked or fitted.

Solid base — a flat surface on the furniture itself or a removable part.

Spring bars — springs mounted on steel bar supports.

Spring twine — twine used for tying the tops of springs in place.

Stuffing iron — a tool used to push stuffing into corners and crevices which cannot be reached by hand.

Tape — flexible steel or cloth tape used for measuring covers and laying out seam lines.

Tow — a flax plant fiber; firm, but not very resilient; inexpensive and easy to work with; used chiefly to provide a firm foundation for other more resilient stuffings.

Trestle — a device to support work at a convenient height.

Tula fiber — a fiber grown in the Southwest; coated with rubber, it makes a strong stuffing; has a spongy appearance.

Upholsterers' tacks — smooth, flat headed tacks; used for all general utility purposes.

Wadding — thin layer of cotton fastened between two sheets of soft paper; used for the same purposes as cotton felt.

Webbing — woven band of coarse jute fibers; used as a base for the pad and as a support for springs.

Webbing stretcher — a lever type tool to stretch webbing and hold it while it is tacked in place.

Webbing tacks — special long tacks for fastening webbing.

Glossary of Wood Finishing Terms

Abrasives — coated papers or cloth, steel wool, pumice stone, or rottenstone, used for cutting down finished surfaces or preparing new wood for finishing.

Adhesion — chemical affinity of any finish coat for the one next below.

Binder — the residue left after the evaporation of the thinner or solvent from a paint, varnish, enamel, or lacquer film.

Bleach — one or more water solutions to remove foreign stains or all natural color from wood surfaces.

Borax — used as a second-coat water solution to neutralize oxalic acid bleach on wood; prevents pink shades on oak or maple.

Brush cleaner — a varnish-remover solvent, or water solution of one or more phosphates in which the brush is soaked; remover is by far the safest method for bristles.

Burning in — the process by which colored-to-match stick shellacs are melted in and polished, to repair damaged surfaces of furniture finishes.

Cement — a material used in repairing furniture finishes when dented.

Drips — a term designating the sagged portions of a finish on table edges and vertical surfaces of furniture.

Drying — a process of losing water or solvents; or the changes by oxidation of a surface film.

Dull finish — a rubbed surface; or one produced by chemical action of flatting agents in a drying film; a surface without gloss.

Durability — the property of a finish film to resist abrasion, solvents, or light.

Dusting — the method of antiquing a finish by applying rottenstone powder to a wax coating, or the presence of dry particles on a lacquer film left by improper or careless spraying methods.

Feathering — the method of lightly stroking finish coatings using only the brush bristle tips to produce a thin, blending action.

15

Felt — American, English, or Spanish wool pressed to a dense mass; used for rubbing blocks with pumice or rottenstone; hard Spanish is best grade.

Filler — a base preparation composed of silex, colors ground in oil, and a grinding liquid or binder; used to fill wood pores level, preparatory to finishing.

Flow — the property of a paint, varnish, or lacquer film which enables it to level off, free of brush marks; or orange peel if sprayed.

Gum turpentine — turpentine distilled from pine gum versus wood turps from chips from old pine stumps.

Hand rub — use of rubbing felt blocks and pumice or rottenstone by hand, as contrasted with belt or machine methods.

Hard — the condition of a finish which enables it to successfully resist the imprint of a thumb nail under pressure.

Highlighting — a coloring or sanding process, by which portions naturally reflecting the light are accented to increase the effect, in contrast with adjacent darker areas.

Hyposulphite of soda — used in bleaching solutions for woods.

Initial set — the surface hardening of a finish film previous to body drying.

Lacquer — a clear varnish of shellac or gum resins dissolved in quick-drying lacquer thinner; applied with a spray gun.

Naphtha — a series of petroleum, or coal-tar distillates, of indefinite hydrocarbon mixtures.

Natural filler — a paste base free of color containing silex, varnish, oil, and drier.

Pumice — a solidified form of lava froth; a porous aluminum silicate. Best grade is American-ground, Italian pumice. Grades as F (single floated) to FFF (triple floated).

Rag off — the process of wiping off excess stain with rags; or blending color on a surface during a glazing operation.

Remover — a solvent for softening old paint and varnish films. Dissolved paraffin is used as a blanket to hold down evaporation of highly volatile solvents; hence brush strokes should be as few as possible to avoid breaking paraffin film.

Rottenstone — a brown-gray powder, aluminum silicate or clay; mined in England and used as a high-luster polishing agent on finishes or metals. Used as a smutting agent in antiquing work.

Rub — the action of cutting down finish films to a level surface.

Rubbing felt — a good grade of hard Spanish felt.

Running — the condition evidenced when a varnish or enamel sags down in curtains because of temperature or faulty manipulation on a vertical surface. Usually caused by the application of too heavy a coat or by having the finish material too thin.

Sagging — the slipping of a coating material over a wide, but not large, vertical surface.

Sealer coat — a coating applied over filler and stain or similar porous area to allow top coats to flow out smooth or level, and to prevent stain "bleeding" through the finish.

Set — the initial hardening of a varnish or paint film previous to body drying to complete hardness.

Sheen — the luster of a rubbed surface when viewed at a small angle.

Shellac — purified lac resin. Generally cut 4 or 5 pounds in a gallon of denatured alcohol, as 4-pound-cut.

Stain — dyestuffs classified as to spirit, oil or water soluble. Term should not be used in connection with pigments which produce modified paints only.

Steel wool — a special grade of tough steel which is mechanically reduced to graded sizes of metal fibers, having square or cutting edges; used in rubbing down the gloss on finish surfaces ready for recoating, or as a polishing medium in the finer grades on metal surfaces; has leveling properties typical of abrasive papers and is particularly useful in rubbing down shellac finishes between coats.

Stick shellac — colored shellacs in handy stick form for repairing finish damages by melting with heated tools.

Surface drying — a condition whereby a top skin coat forms and allows the body portion of a film to remain soft.

Thinner — a term which is too general; should be used in connection with lacquer reducers only, but now is almost generic.

Tipping off — a method of brush stroking with bristle tips only, to remove bubbles or excess finish material.

Tooth — the condition of a surface prepared by sanding, rubbing with steel wool, etc., so as to afford greater anchorage to succeeding coats. Varnishes do not adhere well to gloss undercoats, hence the need for sanding.

Touch-up — a method of repairing off-color damage with shade coats so as to blend in with the rest of the finish.

Varnish — a transparent coating made from fused gums or resins, oils, and thinners, which dries or hardens by oxidation, as contrasted with lacquers which dry by evaporation only.

Nature of the Upholsterer's Work

Formerly, upholstering included such activities as making drapes, curtains, wall hangings, and mattresses as well as covering furniture with fabrics. Today, however, specialization has brought about a division of labor so that upholstering is usually limited to the manufacture and repair of overstuffed furniture. The making of drapes, curtains, and wall coverings

Fig. 1-2. Mass Production of Furniture (Heritage)

is left to the interior decorator; and the manufacture of matresses is still another specialty.

The establishment of mass production operations further sub-divides the upholstery trade, so that an upholsterer rarely completes an entire piece of furniture. He usually performs one or more operations on an assembly-line basis. The procedures vary in different companies all the way from custom building to strictly mass production methods. See Figs. 1-1 and 1-2.

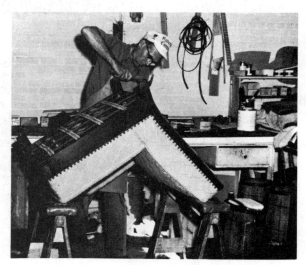

Fig. 1-1. Custom Furniture Manufacturing
(American Furniture)

Furniture Frame Manufacture

The manufacture of the furniture frames is usually a separate operation. One workman may prepare stock using a circular saw, planer, or boring machine, Figs. 1-3 and 1-4. Another may glue stock edge-to-edge all day long as shown in Fig. 1-5. Still another may cut parts on a band saw or round edges on a shaper. Note Figs. 1-6 and 1-7.

A designer may plan and make the master templates for all the wood carvings, and an operator of a gang router may turn out all the

Fig. 1-5. Production Line Gluing of Frame Stock (Kroehler Mfg.)

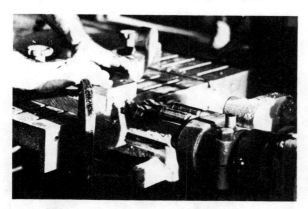

Fig. 1-3. Multiple Horizontal Boring Machine Makes Holes for Dowels (Berkeley)

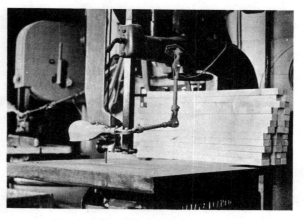

Fig. 1-6. Band Saw, Used for Cutting Irregular Shapes (Berkeley)

Fig.1-4. Multiple Vertical Boring Machine (Berkeley)

Fig. 1-7. Curved Edge Is Made with Shaper (Berkeley)

chair and sofa feet complete with carvings copied from the master template. If no carvings are needed, the feet are turned on a lathe by a lathe operator who may produce on one machine all the feet required for the entire factory's output. Note Fig. 1-8. Parts for various types of chairs and sofas are stored in bins ready for assembly, Fig. 1-9. Other workmen may work entirely on the assembly of the frames: gluing, doweling, and screwing them together. See Fig. 1-10. Spiral-grooved dowels,

Fig. 1-10. Assembling Frame with Power Screwdriver (Berkeley)

Fig. 1-8. Turning Tapered Legs on Mattison Wood Lathe (Kroehler Mfg.)

Fig. 1-11. Machine Sander for Irregular Parts (Berkeley)
Rows of stiff bristles back up shredded sheets of abrasive cloth.

Fig. 1-9. Frame Parts in Storage (Berkeley)

Fig. 1-12. Finish Sanding Grooves — Power Sander Is Used on Flat Surfaces (Berkeley)

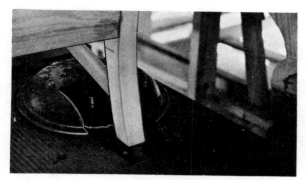

Fig. 1-13. Leg Trimming Table Saw (Berkeley)

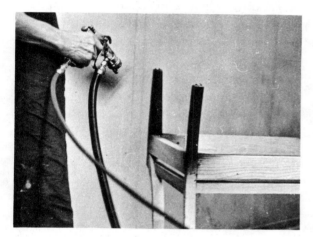

Fig. 1-14. Staining Exposed Legs of Sofa (Berkeley)

Fig. 1-15. Note Turntable and Baffle Panels in Large Spray Booth Chamber (Berkeley)

cut to the required lengths, are dipped in hot hide glue and are driven through matching holes previously drilled on a boring machine.

After being shaped, frame parts which will be visible on the finished furniture are rough sanded by machine and finish sanded both by hand and machine. Note Figs. 1-11 and 1-12. At this stage leg lengths are evenly matched on a special leg trimming saw which cuts off the long leg in a plane with the other three legs, Fig. 1-13.

Another workman then may stain the exposed parts of the wood and lacquer them using spraying equipment, Fig. 1-14. Spray booth chambers are large rooms made of steel plate and sheet metal for fireproofing. Forced air carries excess fumes to the rear of the chamber where they strike large panels down which a continuous layer of water is sprayed. The water carries away the atomized particles keeping the chamber relatively clear. See Fig. 1-15. As a further precaution, workmen wear respirators (masks) to filter the air, thus protecting them from any harmful fumes. Lacquer finishes are sprayed in the same manner after the stain has thoroughly dried. When the legs are finished before they are attached to the frames, smaller drying ovens can be used, as shown in Fig. 1-16.

Fig. 1-16. Drying Prefinished Legs in Oven (Kroehler Mfg.)

Fig. 1-17. Installing Heavy Coil Seat Springs
(American Furniture)

Fig. 1-18. Manufacturing Coil Springs from
Wire Stock (Kroehler Mfg.)

Fig. 1-19. Tacking Arm Pulls in Position (Berkeley)

Upholstery Work

After the frame is constructed, several upholsterers and other specialists may be employed.

The Construction Job

One upholsterer may apply the webbing,
attach the springs, and tack the burlap in place,
Fig. 1-17. Some furniture companies manufacture their own springs, requiring another skilled
worker. See Fig. 1-18. The operations of sewing
or tacking rolled edging in place, applying
the stuffing materials, and attaching the fabrics
are usually performed by the same upholsterer,
Figs. 1-19 and 1-20. Then he is held responsible
for the contour and firmness of the chair as
well as the appearance of the covering material.
In upholstering sofas, some companies use
hydraulic presses to make the application of
outer fabrics easier and quicker. Fig. 1-21
shows a hydraulic back press used for upholstering backs. Final hand sewing of covers may
be performed by persons who are skilled in this
operation. See Fig. 1-22.

Fig. 1-20. Tacking Fabric for Back in Position
(Berkeley)

A specialist called a cutter decides on the layouts of the required pieces of covering used for each piece of furniture. The efficiency of this single operation may determine whether a company makes or loses money. In custom work, the cutter cuts out each piece of fabric individually, while in mass production it is possible for him to cut some fabrics in layers producing many pieces at one cutting. Note Figs. 1-23 and 1-24.

Furniture Cushions

Sewing cushion cases is a separate operation usually performed by women, Fig. 1-25. Women are also employed to sew up the opening on cushions after they have been stuffed or to sew in zippers when these are used.

Fig. 1-21. Hydraulic Back Press, Used in Upholstering Backs (Kroehler Mfg.)

Fig. 1-23. Cutting Fabric in Custom Shop (American Furniture)

Fig. 1-22. Sewing with Curved Needle (Berkeley)

Fig. 1-24. Cutting Multiple Layers with Production Hand Table Cutter (Kroehler Mfg.)

Various methods are used in stuffing cushions, and these will determine the product's quality and cost. Some upholstered pieces have muslin or burlap covered spring units, surrounded on all sides, top, and bottom by cotton batting. To distribute the pressure more evenly on the spring unit, others may have a layer of sisal or rubberized hair on the top and bottom of the spring unit, plus insulators outside the sisal or hair, and then the cotton batting. All of the stuffing materials are arranged in a cushion

stuffing machine and compressed by power, as shown in Fig. 1-26. The cushion case is held at the front of the machine and the whole unit is forced into the case. See Fig. 1-27. The cushion is then ready for hand sewing of the end.

When molded foam rubber units are used in cushions, they are inserted by hand. When soft pillow cushions are made of down, feathers, kapok or a mixture of these, the materials

Fig. 1-25. Sewing Burlap Cover of Spring Units
(American Furniture)

Fig. 1-27. Inserting Spring Unit into Cushion Case
(Berkeley)

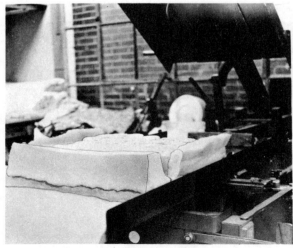

Fig. 1-26. Spring Unit, Padded with Cotton Batting,
Enters Cushion Stuffing Machine (Berkeley)

Fig. 1-28. Weighing Down for Soft Pillow Cushions
(Berkeley)

Fig. 1-29. Finished Chairs Ready for Crating and Shipping (Berkeley)

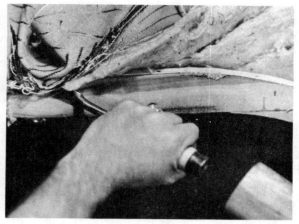

Fig. 1-30. Stripping Old Materials with Ripping Tool and Mallet

for each cushion are first carefully weighed and then transferred to a muslin case by a vacuum and large flexible hose. Fig. 1-28 illustrates the weighing of down for soft pillows. This enclosed unit is then covered with the upholstery fabric case. Sometimes this is done in one operation with a special cushion stuffing machine for soft cushion filling.

The application of the outside covers and the cambric on the bottom of the furniture piece is the last operation. Not being very difficult, it is usually performed by an apprentice or beginner in the trade. The cycle is completed when the new furniture is crated for shipment. See Fig. 1-29.

Reupholstery Work

In re-upholstering, first the furniture is fumigated in an airtight chamber by exposing it to toxic fumes. Fumigation is done for the protection of both customers and workmen. The next operation is stripping the frame, which, because of its simplicity, is usually performed by an apprentice. The *stripper*, as he is called, merely removes all the old tacks using a ripping tool, or ripping hammer, being careful not to split the frame or to damage any exposed woodwork. Note Fig. 1-30.

After the chair is stripped, any needed repairs to the frame are made, such as regluing joints, adding new track rails, or reinforcing the corners. The refinishing of the exposed woodwork is usually done next, although sometimes this is left until the piece of furniture is completely reupholstered. When left until later there is less likelihood that the finish will become scratched; however, some stain or other finishing material accidentally might get on the fabric.

Once the frame has been repaired and refinished, the same procedure is followed as in new construction. Webbing is tacked to the bottom of the seat rails and the front of the back rails; the springs are sewed in place on the webbing and tied in position with spring cord; burlap is tacked in place and stuffing materials are securely attached; the fabrics are stretched and tacked in position; the cushion is made; cambric is tacked to the bottom; and finally any trim such as gimp or fringe is added.

In custom shops, an upholsterer still performs most or all of the operations in the repair of upholstered furniture. Yet even in the small shop a limited degree of specialization often takes place with the owner and more experienced upholsterers performing the more important jobs and the new hands doing the less intricate tasks.

Mass production methods enable the upholsterer to become more proficient at a limited number of operations. This permits a number of upholsterers to turn out more work as a group than they could if each worked on an individual basis, thus lowering the cost of production and the price to the consumer. However, it makes the job less interesting for the upholsterer, and he must be satisfied to be a member of a team. Individual pride of workmanship must be replaced to some extent with pride in group accomplishment.

Statistics of the Trade

The manufacture of upholstered household furniture is identified as a growth industry by the U.S. Department of Commerce having had a 25 percent increase in employment from 44,800 to 56,000 between the years 1947 and 1954. The value added by furniture manufacture (the difference between the value of shipments of furniture plants and their cost of materials, supplies, fuel, and power) amounted to 313 million dollars in 1954. The total value of shipments (the net selling value, f.o.b. plant) from upholstered household furniture manufacturing plants in 1954 was 632.8 million dollars.[1] Of this total, 31.2 million dollars was the value for wood furniture frames for household furniture and 131 million dollars was the value of convertible sofas, jackknife sofa beds, studio couches, and chair beds (excluding chairs sold as part of suites).[2]

In addition to the original manufacture of upholstered furniture, the repair or reupholstery of furniture is an extensive service industry. In 1950 there were 15,823 reupholstery furniture repair establishments having total receipts of $226 million and about one third of these establishments had an annual payroll of $48.8 million. The total number of paid employees was 73,065. In addition to these companies, in the same year there were 68,798 active proprietors of unincorporated businesses. Adding the number of paid employees and the number of proprietors gives a total of 141,863 persons engaged in the repair of household furniture.[3]

A comparison of the number of upholsterers with the numbers of other skilled craftsmen may be made by looking at the census figures. In 1950 there were 61,161 upholsterers (55,942 male and 5,219 female) in the United States.[4]

Occupations of Craftsmen, Foremen and Kindred Workers.[5]

	Male	Female	Total
Bookbinders	13,684	17,487	31,171
Cabinetmakers	72,224	1,064	73,288
Carpenters	907,728	4,809	912,537
Compositors and Typesetters	164,366	11,077	175,443
Electricians	307,013	2,217	309,230
Automobile Mechanics	646,525	4,082	650,607
Molders, Metal	59,879	667	60,546
Plumbers and Pipe Fitters	275,892	1,972	277,864
Shoemakers and Repairers, except factory	54,969	2,149	57,118
Tinsmiths, Coppersmiths and Sheet Metal Workers	121,660	1,163	122,823
Toolmakers and Die Makers and Setters	151,587	1,059	152,646

[1]U.S. Department of Commerce. *Growth Industries in Wood Products and Furniture, Industry Trend Series — No. 6.* Washington, D.C.: Superintendent of Documents, Government Printing Office, Nov. 1957., p. 5.
[2]Ibid., p. 8.

[3]U.S. Department of Commerce. *Statistical Abstract of the United States 1960, 81st Annual Ed.* Wash. D.C.: Superintendent of Documents, U.S. Government Printing Office. Table No. 1152 Selected Services, by Kind of Business: 1954 and 1958. p. 853.
[4]U.S. Department of Commerce. *Statistical Abstract of the United States 1957:* Wash. D.C. Superintendent of Public Documents, U.S. Government Printing Office. Table No. 262, p. 216.
[5]Ibid., Table No. 262, p. 215.

chapter 2

Tools and Equipment for Upholstering

In contrast to many arts or trades, upholstery requires only a few fundamental tools and a minimum amount of equipment. A few hand tools and a pair of trestles to elevate the work to a comfortable working position can set one up for business. It is a false economy to purchase cheap tools when so few are required and they last so long.

Upholsterers' Hammers

Since upholstery requires so many tacking operations, the special upholsterer's hammer is an essential tool. It has a 12-inch hickory handle and a curved head, $5\frac{1}{2}$ inches long. The larger end of the head is solid, and its $\frac{1}{2}$-inch-diameter face is used for driving the tacks home. The other end of the curved head is split and has a 5/16th-inch face. This split end is magnetized for holding and starting the tacks. Notice in Fig. 2-1 that this slit or wedge-shaped core is filled with plastic material. This material prevents the accumulation of dirt, and any subsequent mouth sores that could result from the upholsterer putting this end in his mouth to receive tacks which he stores there. The solid core also increases the magnetic life of the hammer. As a further means of prolonging this magnetic life, a small metal cap is placed on the face of the split end. This should be removed before using, but may be replaced when the hammer is not in use. Waxing the head with a paste wax will prevent rusting.

The curved head enables the upholsterer to tack in deep corners while the small, smooth-edged face permits him to tack gimp in place without marring the woodwork or cutting the fabric. The side of the hammer, which is usually flat, is used for knocking out tacks that are only partially driven in, such as those employed in slip tacking. The side of the hammer is often used also to pound stuffing into position.

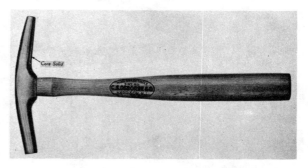

Fig. 2-1. Nine-Ounce Upholsterers' Hammer
(C. S. Osborne)

Webbing Stretchers

Webbing is stretched taut by using either webbing stretchers or webbing pliers. The webbing stretcher most commonly used consists of a hard wooden block 3½ inches wide and 6½ inches long, shaped for easy grasping. It has six steel points on one end to pierce the webbing, and corrugated rubber on the other end to prevent it from slipping or from marring any finished wood. See Fig. 2-2.

Webbing Pliers

Webbing pliers are also used to stretch webbing, Fig. 2-3. Although not as handy as the webbing stretcher, they are better for stretching short pieces of webbing and re-stretching loose webbing. The jaws, 3½ inches wide, are corrugated to improve the gripping quality. A narrow type with 1½-inch jaws is used for re-stretching loose webbing. One end

of the handle sometimes has a claw for removing tacks.

Ripping Tool

The ripping tool is used in the stripping operation for removing old tacks. It is between 7 and 8 inches long and has a blunt chisel edge to get under the tack heads. The metal end has two bends in it so that when the chisel edge is flat against the wood the handle is at a slight angle, providing a comfortable working position for the hand and clearance for the knuckles. The handle, which is about 4 inches long, is made to fit the palm of the hand and may be of wood, usually hickory, or plastic. If made of wood it should have a metal ferrule on each end to prevent splitting when it is hit with a mallet. Note Fig. 2-4. A ripping tool with a plastic handle is more durable.

Claw Tool

If one has a ripping tool, the claw tool is not essential. However, beginners may find that the claw tool has less tendency to slip past the tack since it has a notch in the center of the chisel edge of the blade. See Fig. 2-5. Most upholsterers prefer the ripping tool as it has no notch in which the tacks may jam.

Fig. 2-2. Webbing Stretcher (C. S. Osborne)

Fig. 2-3. Webbing Pliers (C. S. Osborne)

Fig. 2-4. Ripping Tool (C. S. Osborne)

Fig. 2-5. Claw Tool (C. S. Osborne)

Fig. 2-6. Rawhide Mallet (C. S. Osborne)

Mallets

Upholsterers use rawhide, wooden, or rubber mallets to drive either a ripping or claw tool in the stripping operation, Fig. 2-6. They may be procured in various weights from 10 to 20 ounces.

Shears

On both upholsterer's and tailor's shears, the handles are bent up making them easier to use on a flat table, as shown in Fig. 2-7. It is advisable to buy heavy duty shears since they are used to cut burlap and webbing as well as heavy covering fabrics. The shears vary in length from 7 to 12 inches and have cutting lengths from $3\frac{1}{8}$ to $6\frac{1}{4}$ inches. Twelve-inch shears with a $6\frac{1}{4}$-inch cut are recommended. In mass production shops, electric cutters can cut through many layers of fabric at the same time.

Measuring and Layout Tools

A flexible tape is most convenient for measuring, especially around irregular surfaces or curved contours. A steel tape or a good grade cloth tape that won't stretch should be used. A straight yardstick is useful when pieces of fabric are laid out. Tailor's wax or chalk sharpened to a chisel point is used in marking the pattern onto the fabric.

Needles

The upholsterer uses several different types of needles. Even though the trend is to eliminate as much hand sewing as possible by using pre-formed edging materials and metal clips, there still remains considerable hand sewing for which special needles are required.

Straight needles used by upholsterers include both the single point and the double point. Note Fig. 2-8. The double-pointed needles can be used to sew through the material and come back without being turned around. Thus they save time in an operation such as sewing springs to webbing. Single-pointed styles come in lengths from 6 to 12 inches, while double-pointed needles are 6 to 18 inches long. Both styles come with round or triangular points. The triangular points, or spear points as they

Fig. 2-9. Curved Needle with Round Point
(C. S. Osborne)

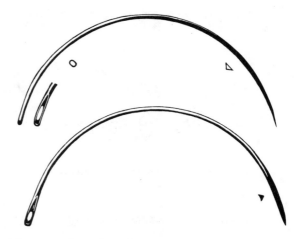

Fig. 2-10. Curved Needles with Triangular Points, Alternate Eye Positions (C. S. Osborne)

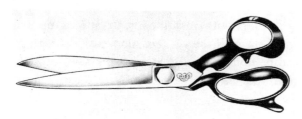

Fig. 2-7. Shears (J. Wiss)

Fig. 2-8. Straight Needles (C. S. Osborne)
A. Single point   B. Double pointed

are sometimes called, are best for sewing leather since they pierce the leather most easily.

Curved needles are used a great deal by the upholsterer. They come with both round and triangular points and in both light and heavy gauges. See Figs. 2-9 and 2-10. The light gauge needles are used on cover fabrics. Curved needles vary in length from 2 to 10 inches, measured along the circumference.

Packing needles, Fig. 2-11, are used for heavy sewing. They are made of heavy gauge steel and have a straight body with a slightly curved spear point. Their lengths vary from 3 to 10 inches.

Regulators

Regulators are similar to needles only they are heavier. See Fig. 2-12. They come in heavy

Fig. 2-11. Packing Needle (C. S. Osborne)

Fig. 2-12. Upholsterers' Regulators (C. S. Osborne)
A. American Pattern   B. English Pattern, with Eye

Fig. 2-13. Upholsterers' Pin or Skewer
(C. S. Osborne)

Fig. 2-14. Two Types of Stuffing Irons
(C. S. Osborne)

and light gauges and range from 6 to 12 inches in length. They are used to smooth irregularities in stuffing materials under a muslin or temporary cover. They are never used through the cover fabric as they might leave holes. A light gauge, 10-inch regulator is the most convenient.

Pins or Skewers

An upholsterer's pin or skewer is a short piece of wire, 3 to 3½ inches long, pointed on one end, and with a round loop on the other end. Note Fig. 2-13. These pins are used to position fabric prior to tacking or sewing, and it is convenient to have two or three dozen.

Stuffing Rod

The stuffing rod, or stuffing iron as it is sometimes called, is a stiff piece of steel 18 inches long. It is used to force stuffing into corners that are difficult or impossible to reach by hand, Fig. 2-14.

Production Tools

To speed up work on a production basis, a spring loaded *hand stapler* or a *stapler hammer* may be employed. See Fig. 2-15. Another tool frequently used in production work is the *Klinch-It tool* which fastens springs to webbing or burlap with metal clips. It speeds up the work since all the work in mounting the springs can be done from the top side. A third production tool is the *hog-ring pliers,* as seen in

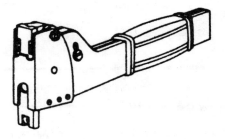

Fig. 2-15. Stapler Hammer (Upholstery Supply)

Fig. 2-16. This is a special pliers designed to hold and close metal rings or clips. It is useful in attaching springs to burlap and in fastening formed rolled edging in place. It is loaded with a supply of rings similar to a hand stapler. Another hand tool made for production work is the *spring clip pliers.* See Fig. 2-17. It is made to fasten either three- or five-prong metal clips to the top edge of seat springs and the wire edge which goes around the edge of the seat. The clips hold the springs to the wire edge providing a straight edge to the seat. See Fig. 2-18.

Common Wood Tools

In addition to the special upholstery tools, the following common hand woodworking tools will be found useful in repairing frames: back saw; try square; T bevel; hand drill with set of twist drills; hand brace with 3/8-inch auger bit, screwdriver bit, countersink bit; and a variety of clamps such as bar clamps, hand screws, and C-clamps to be used in gluing frames.

Fig. 2-16. Hog Ring Pliers (Mount)

Fig. 2-17. Spring Clip Pliers (Mount)
A. For 3-Prong Clips   B. For 5-Prong Clips

Miter Box Saw

Upholstery classes and the person who plans to do extensive upholstery work at home will find a *miter box saw* extremely useful. Straight and angled cuts for frame parts and corner blocks may be cut on the miter box saw, Fig. 2-19. This tool is an essential for the well equipped home workshop. For the person who only plans a limited amount of upholstery

Fig. 2-18. Spring Clips (Upholstery Supply)

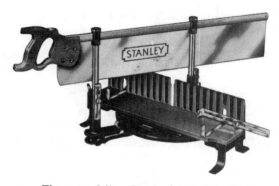

Fig. 2-19. Miter Box and Saw (Stanley)

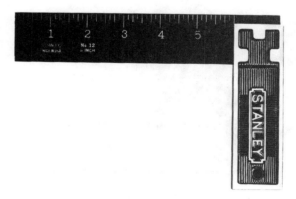

Fig. 2-20. Try Square (Stanley)

work, a *back saw* without the miter box might be sufficient. This could be used in combination with a homemade bench hook on a table or workbench.

Try Square

The try square is used for laying out square cuts and testing corners for squareness,

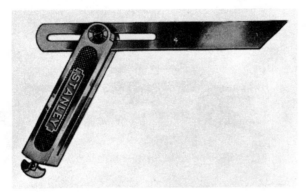

Fig. 2-21. T Bevel (Stanley)

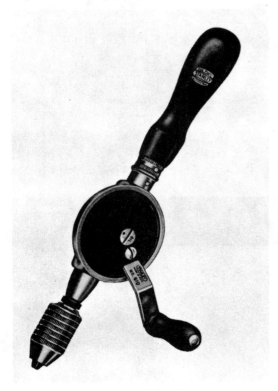

Fig. 2-22. Hand Drill (Stanley)

Fig. 2-20. The blade is graduated in eighths of inches and can be used in measuring the widths of frame parts and the lengths of corner blocks.

T Bevel

The T bevel has an adjustable blade which can be set at any desired angle. See Fig. 2-21. It is extremely useful in transferring angles from the chair to make accurately fitted corner blocks. When the corner block requires a compound angle the T bevel is essential in getting a tight fit.

Hand Drill

The hand drill is used to hold either twist drills or Screwmates for drilling holes for screws. See Fig. 2-22. When *twist drills* are used, it is necessary to use two drills of different sizes to make the holes for each screw. The smaller hole should be the same diameter as the core of the screw, but slightly deeper than its total length. This is extremely important in using hard wood as the screw may break when being inserted if it hits the bottom of the hole. The larger hole should be the same diameter as the diameter of the shoulder of the screw and the same depth as the length of the shoulder. When *Screwmates* (Fig. 2-23) are used, only one bit is necessary. In addition to drilling the

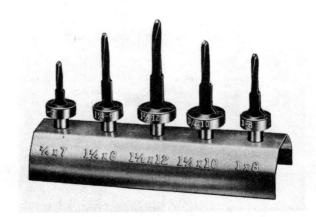

Fig. 2-23. Screwmates (Stanley)

proper screw hole, it also countersinks the top edge of the hole when flat head screws are to be used, all in one operation. Screwmates may be purchased individually or in sets for various sized screws.

Bit Brace

The bit brace is used to hold auger bits for boring holes, countersinks, screwdriver bits, and large drills. See Figs. 2-24 and 2-25. Some types have a ratchet so the brace can be used in corners.

Types of Bits

Countersink bits are used to cut the taper at the top of the hole to match the taper on the underneath side of flat head and oval head screws. See Fig. 2-26. They may be purchased with straight shanks for use in 3-jaw chucks of hand drills or drill presses, or with square tangs for use in bit braces.

Auger bits are used for boring holes in wood, Fig. 2-27. In furniture frame construction, they are useful in boring holes for dowels. Fig. 2-28 pictures a *doweling jig*, useful in getting the hole parallel with the face and

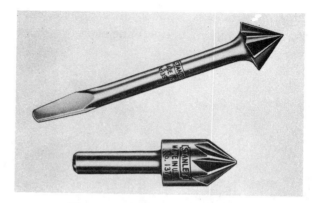

Fig. 2-26. Countersinks (Stanley)

Fig. 2-27. Auger Bits (Stanley)

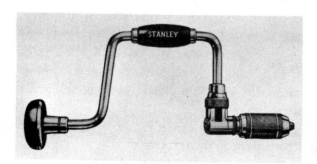

Fig. 2-24. Bit Brace (Stanley)

Fig. 2-25. Screwdriver Bit (Stanley)

Fig. 2-28. Doweling Jig (Stanley)

either perpendicular or at a required angle with the edge or end of a frame member.

Fig. 2-32. Heavy Duty Firmer Chisel (Stanley)

Fig. 2-29. Jack Plane (Stanley)

Fig. 2-30. Block Plane (Stanley)

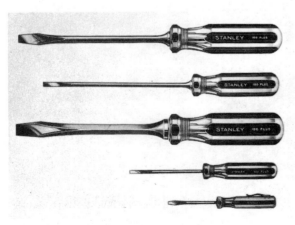

Fig. 2-31. Screwdrivers (Stanley)

Jack Plane

Jack planes are general purpose planes. They come in lengths from $11\frac{1}{2}$ to 15 inches and are used for smoothing edges of boards or removing sharp corners from the edges. See Fig. 2-29.

Block Plane

Block planes are used for planing end grain, Fig. 2-30. They range from $3\frac{1}{2}$ to 7 inches in length. A 6- or 7-inch length is handiest for the upholsterer.

Screwdrivers

Upholsterers should have a variety of different sized screwdrivers, since it is important that the width of the blade fit the length of the slot in the screw. See Fig. 2-31. Screwdrivers with unbreakable plastic handles are recommended as they provide a better gripping surface, especially when grooved.

Chisels

The upholsterer will find a heavy-duty chisel useful in removing excess dried glue and in general cutting. See Fig. 2-32. A chisel with a hard rubber composition handle through which the tang completely extends will withstand heavy usage.

Compasses and Dividers

Compasses are used for laying out small arcs or circles, Fig. 2-33. A pencil is clamped to one leg for marking. Although *dividers* may also be used for scribing small arcs and circles, the lines will have to be gone over with a pencil, Fig. 2-34. Dividers are most helpful to the upholsterer in spacing decorative tacks.

Trestles

Trestles are a special type of bench used by upholsterers to lift the work to a convenient working height. They are used in pairs and their tops should be padded to prevent marring any finished woodwork. A rolled edge is tacked

Fig. 2-33. Compasses (Stanley)

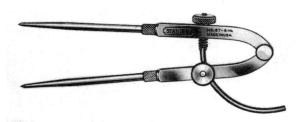

Fig. 2-34. Dividers (Stanley)

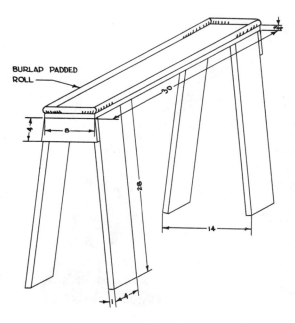

Fig. 2-35. Trestle (Drawn by Alan Brown)

around the top edge to prevent the chairs or sofas from slipping off accidentally. See Fig. 2-35. The tops also provide a convenient place to put tools and small supplies while working.

Sewing Machine

Although satisfactory work can be done on a domestic type sewing machine, it is best to have one with a heavy-duty head such as those usually found in school home economics laboratories. Note Fig. 2-36. A tailor's sewing machine would also be quite satisfactory. It is necessary to have a cording-foot attachment for use in sewing welts which decorate seams and the edges of cushions. See Fig. 2-37. This is not a standard attachment, so it must be purchased separately. One which can be adjusted for either right- or left-hand sewing is most convenient.

Cutting Table

A large table, at least 5 feet wide and 8 feet long, is needed for laying out the fabric and cutting it. Since most upholstery fabric comes in 54 inch widths, the table should be at least 5 feet wide; and the longer the table the better. It should be placed away from any wall so that

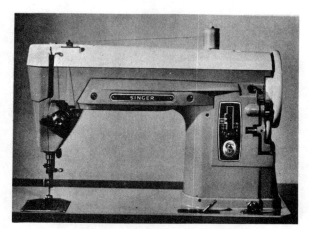

Fig. 2-36. Sewing Machine with Heavy Duty Head (Singer)

one may work at it from all sides. The space underneath may be utilized for storage of fabric and other supplies such as burlap, webbing, rolled edging, and cambric.

Hand Sets

Hand sets or hand irons are made of galvanized sheet iron and are adjustable. See Fig. 2-38. They are used for stuffing cushions by hand, employing a hook and eye closure to compress the box while the cushion cover is slipped over it. In production work, a cushion filling machine is employed. With the increased use of formed foam rubber cushions, cushion filling machines are becoming less essential.

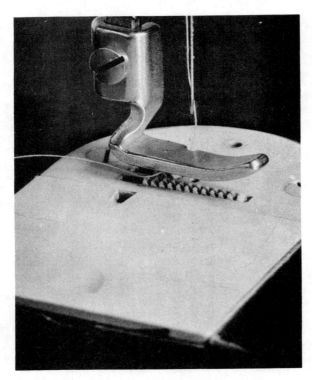

Fig. 2-37. Cording Foot (Singer)

Fig. 2-38. Hand Set for Stuffing Cushions (Lochner Mfg.)

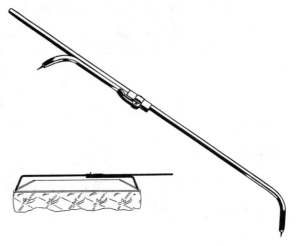

Fig. 2-39. Seam Stretcher, Bar Type (Mount and C. S. Osborne)

Fig. 2-40. Button Covering Machine (Upholstery Supply)

Fig. 2-41. Mechanical Fiber Picker, Covers Removed (Lochner Mfg.)

Seam Stretcher

A seam stretcher is useful in sewing the opening of a cushion after it is stuffed. It consists of a steel, spring tension frame with adjustable chain and hooks for grasping the corners of the cushion to hold the seam tight and straight. See Fig. 2-39.

Button Machine

Hand machines are used for covering buttons with fabric, as shown in Fig. 2-40. They cut the fabric and force it into position around the button. It is not absolutely essential to have a button machine since most upholstery supply companies provide this service at a nominal charge.

Fiber Picker

A machine with toothed rollers may be employed for combing and fluffing such stuffing materials as moss, tow, palm fiber, sisal, hair, and used cotton. See Fig. 2-41. Although this work is often performed by hand in the small shop, the machine is essential in production work since it saves so much time and hand labor.

Construction Materials for Upholstering 3

The materials used in upholstering are obtained from many sections of our own country, as well as from numerous countries throughout the world. Hardwood for furniture frames is produced in the North and Middle Atlantic States. Stuffing materials such as moss and cotton are grown in the Southern States, tow in the Great Lakes Region and Canada, and foam rubber is made in the North Central and North Eastern States. Steel for tacks, springs, and webbing is manufactured in the North Central and Eastern States.

Many upholstering materials are imported from foreign markets. Fibers from the jute plant of India are used in the manufacture of webbing and burlap. Hemp for twine comes from India and Italy. Both England and Italy, in addition to our own country, are large producers of fine stitching twines. England produces the best upholstery needles. Mahogany used for exposed parts of many furniture frames is obtained from South America. Hog hair and horse hair are also procured from South America. Long fiber cotton is imported from Egypt and goose down from Czechoslovakia and Hungary.

Materials such as webbing, burlap, springs, twine, and tacks may be considered construction materials (as well as the materials for the frame construction) since they provide a foundation for the application of the stuffing materials. See Fig. 3-1. The quality of these construction materials will determine the quality and durability of the piece of furniture. It is a false economy to use materials of inferior grades as the small savings effected this way are soon lost when poor materials deteriorate. Since the labor involved is a major consideration, it is foolish to skimp on the quality of the construction materials and thereby cause the job to be redone before it normally should be needed.

Wood for Frames

Construction lumber for frames should be close grained of the hardwood variety, and should possess a medium degree of hardness. The wood must be hard enough to hold the tacks but not so hard that it will be difficult to drive tacks into it. In other words, a tough stringy-grained wood would be quite satisfactory.

The best woods for frames include walnut, mahogany, soft maple, gum, cherry, birch,

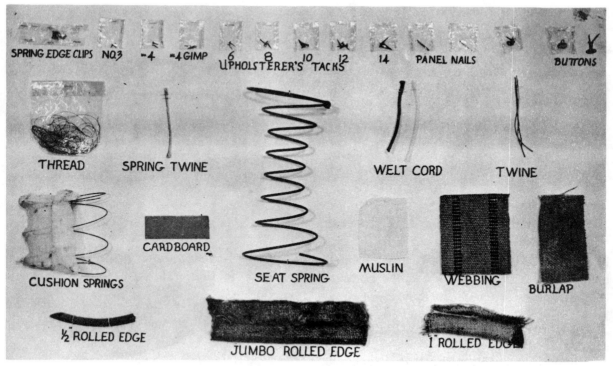

Fig. 3-1. Upholstery Construction Materials

and poplar. Whole frames are seldom entirely of mahogany or walnut because they are too expensive. These costly woods are usually reserved for the exposed parts such as the legs, and, in the case of antiques, the ends of the arms and the top edge of the back. Sometimes maple, cherry, and birch are used similarly for exposed parts only. Parts which will not show after upholstering are then made of less expensive woods such as gum or poplar. Hard maple, yellow pine, and oak are not satisfactory for frames because they are too hard; white pine, on the other hand, is too soft. Woods which tend to split easily, such as redwood and western cedar, should also be avoided. The lumber used for unexposed portions should be straight and relatively free of any large knots which would weaken a part. All lumber used for frames should be well seasoned, preferably kiln dried to a moisture content of less than ten percent.

Webbing

A base for springs and stuffing materials, webbing must be strong enough to bear a great deal of weight once the furniture piece is put into use. There are several types of webbing available.

Jute Webbing

Webbing is a stout, close-woven tape made from coarse jute fibers. It is made in widths of 3, 3½, or 4 inches and in rolls 72 yards long. The 3½-inch width is the most popular commercially, but the person re-upholstering only a few pieces would be wise to buy the 4-inch width. The additional strength gained would be well worth the slight additional cost. The red, blue, or black stripes woven near the edges of the webbing identify its grade. The red striped is the best quality, the blue next, and the black striped the least expensive.

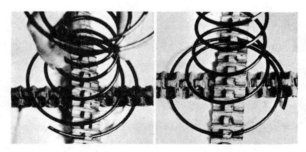

Fig. 3-2. Corrugated and Punched Steel Webbing
(Schramm at Northwest)

Steel Webbing

Steel webbing is available in a variety of types. Widths from ⅝ inch to an inch are made, but the ¾-inch is the most common. Webbing may be either plain, perforated for nails, or corrugated and punched so that springs may be woven through them rather than being sewed. Fig. 3-2 shows this latter type of webbing. Steel webbings are sold under various trade names indicating that they will not sag. This is true, but it also results in less resiliency and a less comfortable piece of furniture. Steel webbing is usually found in the cheaper lines of furniture. Sometimes it can be used to advantage to reinforce a weak piece of webbing as a temporary measure, but even here it would be better to add another piece of jute webbing.

Cotton Webbing

Cotton webbing, a khaki color, may be obtained in such widths as ½, ⅝, 1, 1¼, 1½, and 2 inches. It is used chiefly in reinforcing arms and backs of boudoir furniture, and should never be used as a substitute for jute webbing.

Plastic Webbing

Plastic webbing is being used more frequently in modern furniture, as seen in Fig. 3-3. It comes in a variety of colors and in widths from ¾-inch to 5 inches. Since it resists the elements of weather well, it is widely used for

Fig. 3-3. Plastic Webbing (Upholstery Supply)

lawn and porch furniture; however, prolonged exposure to direct sunlight will cause it to deteriorate.

Tray Webbing

A special webbing is made for the supports on serving trays used by hotels and restaurants. It comes in rolls 100 yards long and 2½ inches wide, and is usually white with a blue stripe.

Burlap

Burlap is a sturdy fabric woven from yarns made of the coarse fibers of jute or hemp. Sometimes in the less expensive grades the fibers of flax are used. It comes in various weights such as 7½, 10, 12, and 16 ounces, and also in different widths such as 36, 40, and 45 inches. The 40-inch width is most common. The 10-ounce weight is most frequently used commercially; however, the 12-ounce weight is recommended for individual use as the added strength is worth the slight difference in price. The extremely heavy 16-ounce weight is used chiefly in combination with steel webbing to give a "sagless" type construction.

Upholstery Springs

Many different types of springs are made for upholstery work. They vary in size, style,

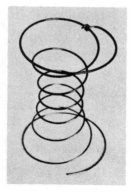

Fig. 3-4. Seat Spring   Fig. 3-5. Pillow Spring
(Schramm at Northwest) (Schramm at Northwest)

wire gauge, and degrees of compression to serve a variety of purposes. Seat springs, for example, need to be heavier and firmer than springs used in arms or backs, while the lightest springs are those used in cushions.

Seat Springs

Heavy coil springs are used for seat springs. They may be sold by the pound or by the individual spring. They are shaped somewhat like an hourglass with the center coils smaller than the end coils. The end coils are open and one end has a bend in it to prevent it from puncturing the burlap. See Fig. 3-4. For this reason the bent end should always be placed up, while the flat end without the bend rests against the webbing. Seat springs range from #00 (11 gauge wire and 4 inches high) to #6 (8 gauge wire and 14 inches high). They come in three degress of compression — soft, medium, and hard — determined by the size of the center coil. The wider the center coil is, the softer the spring will be. The wider centers, or soft and medium, are more frequently used. If extremely heavy persons are to use the furniture, the hard springs (with small centers) would be an advantage.

Soft seat springs should be tied approximately two inches lower than their open height, medium seat springs one inch lower, and hard springs at full open height. The appropriate size may be determined by consulting the following table:

Spring Number	00	0	1	2	3	4	5	6
Height in Inches	4	5	6	8	9½	10½	12	14
Wire Gauge		11	11	11	10½	9½	9½	8½	8

Pillow Springs

Although pillow springs are lighter in weight than seat springs, they are similarly shaped except for a knot at each end. See Fig. 3-5. Generally they are used for arms and backs. The wire gauge for each height follows:

Height in Inches	4	6	8	10
Wire Gauge	14	14	12	12

Cushion Springs

Used for automobile and truck seats, cushion springs come in a 4-inch height made of 11-gauge wire and in a 6-inch height made of 10-gauge wire. They may be purchased with one or both ends tied.

Spring Bars

Spring bars are composed of either three or four conical springs attached at their small ends to a metal bar or support, as shown in Fig. 3-6. The ends of the bar are secured to the top edge of the seat rails and the front edge of the back rails. They vary in length from 16 to 26 inches, in multiples of 2 inches and in height from 4 to 7 inches. The bar supports drop down from the top of the rails 1½ inches. This type of spring is found in cheaper furniture and is used to eliminate webbing and the labor of attaching it and sewing the springs in place. They may sag less than webbing if they don't break, but their lack of resiliency makes them less comfortable.

Fig. 3-6. Spring Bars (Schramm at Northwest)

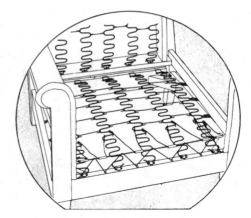

Fig. 3-7. No-Sag Zig-Zag Springs
(Upholstery Supply)

No-Sag Springs

No-Sag springs are made from continuous zig-zag shaped wire. Note Fig. 3-7. Coils 120 feet long (9-gauge wire) are available for seats while those 140 feet long (11-gauge wire) are used for backs. Accessories needed for installing No-Sag springs include E clips, K clips, helical springs, connecting wire links, and one-inch cement or rosin-coated nails. This type of construction is said to save seventy-five percent of the time required for springing up, thus being used primarily in competitively priced furniture.

Cushion Spring Units

Small springs (2½ or 3 inches in diameter and 3½ inches high) are encased in a muslin or burlap sleeve and sewed or clipped together to form cushion spring units. See Fig. 3-8. Use the largest size unit nearest the dimensions of the cushion being made. These units are also used sometimes for backs of chairs and occasionally on the arms of massive furniture.

Fig. 3-8. Cushion Spring Unit
(Schramm at Northwest)

Rubberized Hair

Seat and back foundations are frequently made from rubberized hog's hair manufactured into mat forms or in loose form. See Fig. 3-9. The strength and resiliency of the hog's hair undergoes rigid tests after it is processed.

Spring Twine

Seat springs are tied in position with spring twine. Use the best grade obtainable, as the

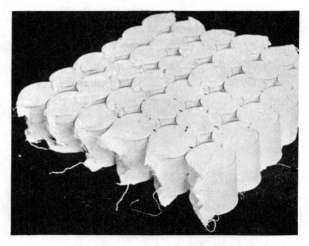

Fig. 3-9. Rubberized Hair — Open, Mesh-Back, and
Foam Rubber Topped (Armour)

life of the job depends upon the life of the twine holding the springs. Six-ply Italian hemp has the reputation for being the strongest, though other good quality hemp twines are probably just as strong. All of the six-ply No. 60 hemp twines will stand over a 200-pound pull. Spring twine has a polished or waxed finish and comes in 1-pound balls, packed six balls to a package; in 5-pound tubes; or in either 9- or 50-pound reels. Lighter weight twine, made of jute or flax, is sometimes used for tying backs because there is less strain. It is advisable for the individual upholstering his own chair to use the six-ply hemp for tying both seat and back springs.

Stitching Twine

Stitching twine, sometimes referred to in the trade as *mattress twine,* is a flax or linen twine used for sewing the springs to the webbing, the burlap to the springs, and the stuffing to the burlap. It is also used for making edge rolls and spring edges. The linen is stronger and only slightly more expensive than the flax. Both come in packages of six, eight-ounce balls.

Upholstery Tacks

Several kinds of tacks are used in upholstering — regular upholsterers' tacks for attaching fabrics; webbing tacks; gimp tacks

for semi-concealed finishing; and fancy tacks for decorative finishing. All upholstery tacks are sterilized because upholsterers commonly store them in the mouth while working. Regular upholsterers' tacks are blued, range in size from No. 1 ($3/16''$) to No. 20 ($15/16''$), and are sold in boxes of $1/8$, $1/4$, 1, 10, 25, or 100 pounds. See Fig. 3-10.

Webbing tacks are similar to upholsterers' tacks except that they have barbs to give them greater holding power. They are made in two sizes, 12 and 14 oz. See Fig. 3-11.

Gimp tacks are blued and have small round heads. Used chiefly in attaching covers, they range in size from No. 2 ($5/16''$) to No. 8 ($10/16''$) and can be purchased in boxes of $1/8$, $1/4$, 1, 10, 25, or 100 pounds. See Fig. 3-12.

Fancy or decorative tacks are used chiefly in covering antiques and with leather or plastic. They may be nickel, lacquered, or brass-plated with an antique, bright, or dull finish. See Fig. 3-13.

Fig. 3-11. Webbing Tacks (Upholstery Supply)

Fig. 3-12. Gimp Tacks (Upholstery Supply)

Fig. 3-13. Fancy Tacks (Upholstery Supply)

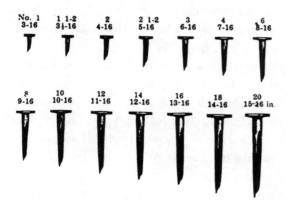

Fig. 3-10. Upholsterers' Tacks (Upholstery Supply)

Styles of Furniture 4

The styles in furniture reflect the history of civilization. They are influenced not only by need, function, and the availability of materials and money, but also by taste, fashion, and manner of living. A thorough study of the styles of furniture would be a lifetime undertaking; therefore, only some of the highlights will be mentioned in this chapter.

In general, furniture styles of today may be broken down into two broad categories — *traditional or period* and *modern or contemporary*. The various European periods were usually named after reigning monarchs or master craftsmen. In America we find such terms as Early and Late Colonial, Federal, American Empire, Modernistic, and Modern or Contemporary.

Factors Affecting Design

Comfort has not always been a factor in designing furniture. The Egyptians made their seats, which were really thrones, from stone, ebony, or ivory. The Romans made theirs from marble and bronze, and the people of the Middle Ages used wood. When a family of the Middle Ages possessed a chair it was generally reserved for use by the head of the family and it became, in a sense, a domestic throne from which he ruled his household. The seats of Medieval chairs were built high from the floor so that the sitter's feet would not touch the cold stone floor and could rest on a footstool. They usually had high backs and sides, not for ornamental purposes, but as protection against cold, wintry drafts which were common to both cottage and castle, especially in the northern countries.

Chairs have varied in form and size to meet the requirements of fashion at different periods in various lands. When the heavy armour of feudal knights gave way to simpler military attire, it was no longer necessary to have such strong, heavy seats. Later, the need for space to accommodate the ladies' hoop skirts or farthingales and the gentlemen's puffed-trunk hose caused the side panels of the chairs to be removed. In Queen Anne's day the arms were foreshortened and set back to allow the full skirts of women to billow becomingly about them. Very high backs were devised as backgrounds and support for tall periwigs of fashionable women.

Styles in American furniture have been influenced by the furniture of many European countries and the Orient. The early colonists reproduced many English designs. The English in turn had been influenced by the Dutch and French. The designs of many countries such as Italy, Spain, Germany, Holland, Denmark, Sweden, and China have been reflected in American furniture styles; however the English and the French designs have been the most predominant.

The Eighteenth Century was the "Golden Age" of furniture designs. Many of our traditional styles are patterned after the work of master craftsmen of this era who successfully combined comfort, utility, elegance, and formality.

English Styles

Fortunately, the early English furniture periods (from the latter part of the Fifteenth Century to the latter part of the Seventeenth Century) had very little influence on American styles in furniture. This period covered the reigns of Henry VII, Henry VIII, Elizabeth, James I, and Charles I. It included the *Gothic, Tudor,* and *Jacobean* styles which were for the most part straight-lined, heavy, massive, and generally unattractive. An English 16th or 17th Century turned arm chair is shown in Fig. 4-1.

The William and Mary Period of the latter part of the Seventeenth Century, known as the "Age of Walnut," was the first English period to have much influence on American furniture designs. This period utilized curved rather than straight lines, and its furniture was more graceful, lighter in weight, and better adapted to human comfort. It provided flat and serpentine stretchers, bun feet, cup turnings, and the Dutch thick, short cabriole leg. For example,

Fig. 4-1. English Turned Oak Arm Chair, 16th or 17th Century (Met. Mus. of Art)

Fig. 4-2. English William and Mary Walnut Chairs, 1688-1702 (Met. Mus. of Art)

note in Fig. 4-2 the walnut William and Mary chairs.

The Queen Anne Period during the early part of the Eighteenth Century continued with curved lines and gave us a longer cabriole leg, club feet, solid splat (center back-piece), broken pediment, and shell carvings.

The Georgian Period was known as the "Golden Age of Furniture." Illustrated in Fig. 4-3 is an early 18th century Georgian arm chair. It was the influence of the great English furniture designers of this 18th century period, such as Chippendale, Hepplewhite, the Adam brothers, and Sheraton, that determined many of the furniture styles in America. Their style is still the basis for much of our "Traditional"

Fig. 4-3. English Early Georgian Walnut Arm Chair, 1715-1720 (Met. Mus. of Art)

Fig. 4-5. English Hepplewhite Arm Chair, 1790 (Met. Mus. of Art)

Fig. 4-4. English Chippendale Mahogany Ladder-Back Chair, 1765-1775 (Met. Mus. of Art)

Fig. 4-6. English Sheraton Arm Chairs, 1790-1795 (Met. Mus. of Art)

or "Period" furniture. The first half of the Eighteenth Century was known as the "Mahogany Age" and the latter half as the "Age of Satinwood." From Chippendale we have the pierced fiddle-back and ladder-back, from Hepplewhite the shield-back, and from Sheraton the rectangular-back chairs and slender tapering or turned fluted legs. See Figs. 4-4, 4-5, and 4-6.

French Periods

American furniture styles were influenced by the French indirectly through the English styles before the American Revolution. After the Revolution the influence was direct and many American designers turned to the Louis XVI and Directoire styles for inspiration. The American Empire designs followed the French Empire styles closely, but fortunately omitted

Fig. 4-7. French Louis XV Walnut Bergére Arm Chair, 1725-1750 (Met. Mus. of Art)

Fig. 4-9. Mahogany Desk Chair, French First Empire Period, 1804-1815 (Met. Mus. of Art)

Fig. 4-8. French Louis XVI Chairs, 1744-1793 (Met. Mus. of Art)

Fig. 4-10. French 19th Century Side Chairs (Met. Mus. of Art)

Fig. 4-11. American Pine and Ash, Slat-Back
Arm Chair, 1650-1700 (Met. Mus. of Art)

Fig. 4-12. American Maple and Oak Side Chair,
1650-1675 (Met. Mus. of Art)

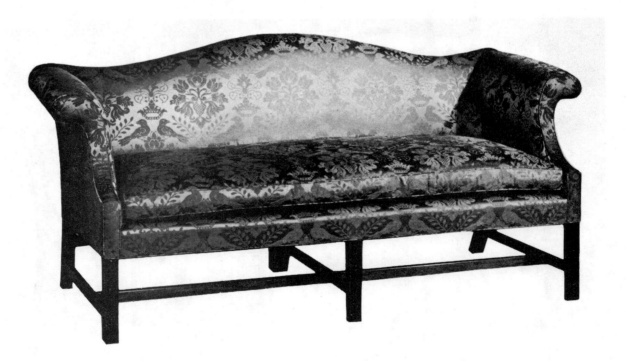

Fig. 4-13. Reproduction of Colonial Williamsburg Sofa (Kittinger)

the use of lions' heads, and many of the Egyptian motifs of the French style. A product of the Louis XV Period (2nd quarter of 18th century) is shown in Fig. 4-7. A later period, the last half of the 18th century, is credited with the Louis XVI chair Fig. 4-8 illustrates. Fig. 4-9 shows a desk chair from the first part of the 19th century, and Fig. 4-10 pictures an example from the last part of that century.

Colonial American Furniture

Early American furniture of the Seventeenth Century tended to be simple and functional. Straight lines predominated, with little decoration except turnings. See Fig. 4-11. Legs were either turned, square, or a combination of both, as shown in Fig. 4-12. Native woods such as ash, maple, pine, and oak were mainly used. Note the original colonial Williamsburg sofa in Fig. 4-13. Toward the end of this century

Fig. 4-15. American (Hepplewhite Style) Mahogany Side Chair, 1775-1800 (Met. Mus. of Art)

Fig. 4-14. American (Hepplewhite-Influenced) Mahogany Arm Chair, 1785-1795 (Met. Mus. of Art)

some mahogany was used and decorations started to include some carvings.

In the Eighteenth Century or late Colonial Period, the use of smooth sweeping curves greatly improved the design of American furniture, Fig. 4-14. In addition to those used earlier, a wider variety of local woods was used, such as cherry, black walnut, hickory, cedar, curly and birds-eye maple. A more extensive use of mahogany also permitted a wider use of decorative carving as seen in Fig. 4-15. The English influence of Chippendale and Hepplewhite was strongly felt in America during this century.

Federal and American Empire Periods

During the late Eighteenth and early Nineteenth Centuries, the English influence continued through the work of the Adam brothers and Sheraton. See Fig. 4-16. After the American Revolution, the English influence was partly replaced by the influence of the French Empire

Fig. 4-16. American Sheraton Arm Chair, 1790-1800 (Met. Mus. of Art)

Fig. 4-18. American Mahogany Lyre-Back Chair, 1805-1815 (Met. Mus. of Art)

Fig. 4-17. Reproduction of Duncan Phyfe Two-Cushion Love Seat (Berkeley)

style, and the American designer Duncan Phyfe came into his own. Fig. 4-17 pictures one of his creations. His tables and chairs with their sweeping curved legs with brass claw feet and his lyre-back chairs were outstanding, Fig. 4-18, and his designs are still in high demand today. In adapting the French Empire styles, American designers wisely omitted excessive details of decorative carvings.

Victorian Period

The last half of the Nineteenth Century was a rather dark period in respect to American furniture design and is referred to as the "Black Walnut and Horsehair Period." The fabric used predominately was woven with black horsehair as the filler and the ends of the hair tended to break through with irritating results. The Machine Age also practically eliminated hand wood carving and promoted monotonous spool turnings and gingerbread fretwork. However, the end of the Nineteenth

and early Twentieth Centuries saw a return to classic designs.

Modern American Furniture

American furniture of today falls into two main categories, the traditional period and the modern or contemporary. The former is still influenced by the designs of the early craftsmen, as can be seen in Figs. 4-19 and 4-20. On the other hand, contemporary furniture design is continually being influenced by new materials, processes, utility, fashion, and mode of living. New materials such as plastic covering material and tubular aluminum have made kitchen, patio, lawn and beach furniture more functional. Note Figs. 4-21 and 4-22. Foam rubber and molded wood frames have enabled the furniture designer to be more versatile as Figs. 4-23 and 4-24 show. Lower ceilings in our homes have tended to reduce the height of

Fig. 4-19. American Chinese Chippendale Wing Chair with Reversible T Cushion (Berkeley)

Fig. 4-20. American Traditional Wing Chair with Fixed Cushion, Cabriole Legs, and Ball and Claw Feet (Berkeley)

furniture for better proportions and appearance, Fig. 4-25. Small apartments and the desire for changes in furniture arrangements have brought about an increased use of sofa beds as well as sectional furniture that can be used in many different combinations and arrangements.

Fig. 4-23. Plastic Covered Club Chair, Reversible T Cushion (Masland)

Fig. 4-21. Tubular Steel Kitchen Chair, Plastic Upholstered (Loyal Metal)

Fig. 4-22. Body-Contour Chair (Lumite)

Fig. 4-24. Contemporary Boudoir Chair (Lumite)

Fig. 4-25. Contemporary Lounge Chairs Covered with Woven Saran Fabric (Lumite)

Summary of English Furniture Styles

Style — Designer	Sovereign	Predominant Woods
Gothic	Henry VII	Oak
Tudor Elizabethan	Henry VIII Elizabeth I	Oak
Jacobean	James I, Charles I	Oak

William and Mary	William and Mary
	    Influenced by Dutch styles which had been influenced by Spanish styles
		Walnut
		    "The Age of Walnut"

Queen Anne	Queen Anne	Walnut and Mahogany

Early Georgian and Georgian	George I, II, III
	    "The Golden Age of Furniture"
		Mahogany, Walnut, Satinwood
		    "The Age of Mahogany"
		    "The Age of Satinwood"

Thomas Chippendale	England's most versatile, celebrated furniture designer and wood carver	Preferred Mahogany. Used French polishing
George Hepplewhite	A lighter, more delicate style than Chippendale's	Satinwood
Adam brothers Robert and James	Architects and furniture designers who subordinated the importance of carving	Mahogany, Satinwood, Inlays with Holly, Ebony and Tulip Painted Panels of Pine and Lime Wood
Thomas Sheraton	Last of the great English furniture designers; second only to Chippendale in influence and importance	Satinwood, Rare Wood Inlays
Regency "Late Georgian"	George IV	Mahogany, Rosewood, Satinwood Tulipwood
Victorian	Victoria	
William Morris	Famous for his adjustable back Morris chair with removable seat and back cushions	

Period	Style Characteristics
1485 - 1509	Straight lines, massive and very heavy. Ex., trestle tables, stools, chests.
1509 - - 1603	Straight lines and massive, but more formal. Ex., bulbous ornaments, Tudor rose, carving, paneling.
1603 - 1649	Straight, sturdy, squat, heavier and more ornate than Tudor, turned, carved, twisted wood. Ex., early gate leg and refectory tables, wainscot chairs, cupboards, paneling, carving, moldings and ornaments.
1688 - 1702	Curved lines, lighter, graceful, adapted to human comfort. Ex., flat and serpentine stretchers, bun feet, cup turnings, hood tops on chairs and settees, Dutch thick short cabriole leg.
1702 - 1714	Curved lines. Ex., cabriole legs, club feet, solid splat, broken pediment, shell carvings.
1714 - 1806	Heavier and more solid than Queen Anne. Ex., casters on chair and table feet, carved cabriole legs with claw and ball feet, hoof and paw feet, furniture upholstered with mohair, silk, velvet and tapestry.
1740 - 1775	Pierced splat variation of fiddle back, ribbon backs, ball and claw foot, rarely used turning. Influenced by French, Chinese and Gothic designers.
1760 - 1786	Serpentine curve, straight tapering legs, spade feet, shield-back, oval-back.
1760 - 1795	Simplicity, elegant slenderness, low relief. Used the urn, laurel leaf, the acanthus, the ribbon band, and the garland. Influenced Sheraton and Hepplewhite.
1790 - 1806	Delicate, slender motifs, vertical lines, long sweeping curves. Used narrow tapering or slender, turned, fluted legs. Famous for square or rectangular backs with back legs extended to meet the top rail.
1811 - 1830	Simplicity of design, sophisticated style, ornament restricted and severe with an absence of carving.
1837 - 1850	Squat, writhing lines. Mixtures of styles. No distinguishing features. Attempted to develop a workable philosophy of furniture design based on a consideration of the material, function, and method of construction as a control of form and character.
1834 - 1896	

Summary of French Furniture Styles

Style — Designer	Sovereign		Predominant Woods
Gothic			Oak, Pine, and Chestnut
French Renaissance	Charles VIII Louis XII Francois I Henry II, IV Louis XIII	1453 - 1498 1498 - 1515 1515 - 1547 1547 - 1610 1610 - 1643	Walnut
Quatorze Andre Charles Boulle	Louis XIV Architect, painter, carver in mosaic, artist in cabinet work, chaser, inlayer, and designer		Walnut, Ebony
Regency	Philip Duke of Orange		Walnut, Mahogany Rosewood
Quinze	Louis XV		Mahogany, Walnut, Ebony, Oak, Cherry, Beech, Elm and Fruit Tree Woods
Seize	Louis XVI		Walnut, Mahogany, Satinwood
French Provincial	Louis XIV, XV, XVI		Oak More Than Walnut
Directoire (Directory)	Directors governed from 1795 - 1799		Walnut, Mahogany, Satinwood
Empire	Napoleon I		Mahogany, Ebony

Period	Style Characteristics
12th, 13th 14th centuries	Straight lined, heavy and massive. Gothic treatment confined to decoration; construction little affected by Gothic style. Trefoil and quatrefoil were chief motifs in wood carving. Lion paws, heavy stretchers.
1453 - 1643	Classically graceful, unique carving, Italian motifs. Ornament subordinate to design but used profusely; shell design used extensively. Turning, inlay. Upholstery extensive with velvet and brocade.
1643 - 1715	Sumptuous extravagant furniture. Straight and massive in scale; ornate, using shells, scrolls, acanthus foliage, cloven hoofs, ram's head, metal mounts, brass nails. Chairs formal and high-backed, both carved and upholstered, straight and curved stretchers, inlay and marquetry.
1710 - 1735	Modified Louis XIV forms. Less severe curves, blending artistic restraint with delicate movement. Pierced carving of foliage and ribbons on chair backs.
1715 - 1774	Sweeping curves, ornate decorations, broken shell, curled endive, spiral scroll, cabriole leg with French scroll foot, carving, inlay, veneering, painting, gilding, metal mounts.
1774 - 1793	Straight lines, small in scale, classic in detail. Chair backs carved or upholstered; legs straight, fluted, turned or carved with classical motifs, urns, pendant husks, lyres, oak leaves, acanthus leaf, and the acorn. Ornament was a means rather than an end.
1710 - 1795	Simple, graceful, functional and uncluttered. Omitted the ornateness of the Louis XIV and Louis XV periods, but retained the elegance of line.
1795 - 1804	Added Revolutionary emblems to Louis XVI pieces such as triumphal arches, Liberty caps, spirit levels, pikes, oaken boughs, clasped hands and tables of the law.
1799 - 1814	Cold, formal, full of dignity. Simple types were beautiful, but final development was clumsy and grotesque. Plain columns and claw feet most used. Roman and Greek emblems used lavishly. The wreath and torch, Roman eagle, Athenian bus, Greek fret, honeysuckle and Egyptian sphinx were used.

Summary of American Furniture Styles

Style — Designer	Historical Event		Predominant Woods
Early Colonial	Jamestown Colony Landing of Pilgrims	1607 1620	Oak Pine
Late Colonial	American Revolution	1776	Oak, Black Walnut, Curly, Plain and Birds-Eye Maple, Birch, Ash, Hickory, Cherry, Cedar, Pine
Federal Duncan Phyfe	Post Revolution Period		Black Walnut, Mahogany
American Empire	American designers followed the French Empire style, but omitted lions' heads, griffins and many incongruous Egyptian details		Mahogany, Curly Maple, Rosewood, Cherry, Walnut, Fruit Woods
Victorian	Westward migration "Black Walnut and Horsehair Period"		Black Walnut, Oak, Rosewood

Transitional
  Art Nouveau (Fr.)
  Arts and Crafts (Eng.)
  Jugendstil and
    Secession (German)
	Chicago Fair
	"Gay Nineties"
		1890	Bird's-Eye Maple, Cherry, Red Mahogany, Oak

Modernistic	International Exposition of Modern Decorative and Industrial Arts at Paris. Americans shocked at discovering they had nothing distinctly "American" to exhibit in the furniture line.		Mahogany, Walnut, Maple, Cherry, Oak, Birch
American Modern or Contemporary			Mahogany, Walnut, Oak, Maple, Cherry, Finished Natural

Period	Style Characteristics
1607 - 1725	Simple, plain, functional. Styled after the English Gothic which was still prominent in the English cottage furniture. The furniture was heavy and sturdy with the emphasis on function and only a little attention to design. Ex., pine settees, wainscot chairs, gate-leg tables, chests.
1725 - 1790	Influenced at first by the English Jacobean style and later by the William and Mary, Queen Anne and Georgian styles. American designers were greatly influenced by Chippendale and Hepplewhite near the end of this period. Ex., ladder-back and Windsor chairs, highboys, lowboys, corner cupboards, four-poster beds.
1790 - 1825	Adam and Sheraton influence felt. After the Revolution some Americans turned to the French Louis XVI and Directory styles. Ex., chairs, tables, sofas.
1812 - 1830	Massive but well designed. Liberal use of smooth flowing, sweeping curves, flared legs. Curved columns, lion or eagle claw feet, pineapple finials, ornamental brass, and glass drawer pulls. Ex., sofas, pedestal tables, gondola, sleigh, and four-poster beds.
1840 - 1890	Machine age practically eliminated carving and brought in spool turning and fret work. Little esthetic discernment. Gothic influence in 40's and 50's. Also interest in medievalism. Ex., jagged work on house gables, lacy appendages on tables and chairs.
1890 - 1925	Return to classicism — Louis XIV and French Empire. Arts and crafts of William Morris found a native style in Spanish Missions in California. Designs quite ornate and clumsy. Use of hammered copper and burnt leather.
1925 - 1935	Triangular shapes, sharp corners, straight lines. Return to plain surfaces. Simplicity predominant feature.
1935 - present	Streamlining, rounded corners, low lines. Ex., tubular steel chairs, molded wood frames.

Designing and
Reconditioning Furniture Frames 5

The comfort and durability of an upholstered piece of furniture begin with a well
designed, sturdy frame. Most furniture is
patterned to meet the needs of persons of
an average height of 5 feet, 8 inches. A well
built frame should outlast several fabric covers.

Design

A chair should be designed to fit the type
of person who is going to use it. If he is the
lounging type, a chair that he can slide down
into will please him. However, if he sits stiff
and erect, a more formal style will be to his
liking. The height of a seat from the floor
should be about 14 or 15 inches for the lounge
chair and 15 or 16 inches for more formal types.
Dining room chairs are usually 18 inches from
the floor.

The depth of the chair (the distance from
the front edge of the seat to the back) should
be at least 20 inches while 22 inches is better.
In the case of a heavily cushioned chair or a
lounging chair for a person with long legs, the
depth should be increased to 24 inches. A slight
($1/2$ to $1\frac{1}{2}$ inch) backward slope of the seat
from the front to back increases comfort. The
width of the seat (the distance between the
arms) should be a minimum of 20 inches, and,
of course, greater for stout persons.

Types of Frames

The types of frames used in seating furniture are almost limitless especially with their
many possible modifications. Dining room chair
frames are generally classified by the types of
backs used and also by whether or not arms are
included. Some typical styles of backs used in
dining room chairs include the ladder-back,
the shield-back, the lyre-back, the slat-back, and
the fiddle-back. See Figs. 5-1 through 5-5. Those
having arms, known as arm chairs, are used by
the master of the household, while those without arms are called side chairs and are used by
other family members.

Wooden kitchen chairs of yesteryear have
been largely replaced by tubular steel or aluminum frames using plastic covering materials.

Frames for living room chairs and sofas
are frequently determined by the styles of the
backs or cushions or in some cases by a particular function. Some typical backs include the
tufted-back, the pillow-back, the barrel-back,

the channel-back, and the wing chair. See Figs. 5-6 through 5-10. Modifications and combinations add to the numerous types, such as the wing channel-back. Backs may also be plain or have buttons. The cushions may be fixed (non-removable) or reversible, Fig. 5-11. They may also be rectangular, tapered, or oddly shaped such as the T cushion. In sofa frames there are the single, double, triple, and even the four-cushion styles. The function of the sofa may also determine the type of frame. Examples are the sofa bed, the gossip seat, and the love seat. Note Figs. 5-12 and 5-13.

Fig. 5-3. American Banister-Back Arm Chair, 18th Century (Met. Mus. of Art)

Fig. 5-1. Ladder-Back Chippendale Arm and Side Chairs (Hickory Chair)

Fig. 5-4. Solid Slat-Back Arm and Side Chairs (Hickory Chair)

Fig. 5-2. Hepplewhite Shield-Back Arm and Side Chairs (Hickory Chair)

Fig. 5-5. Duncan Phyfe Fiddle-Back Arm and Side Chairs (Hickory Chair)

Fig. 5-6. Club Chair with Tufted Back and
Reversible T Cushion (Hickory Chair)

Fig. 5-8. Barrel-Back Chair with Fixed Cushion
(Masland)

Fig. 5-7. Club Chair with Pillow Back and
Reversible T Cushion (Hickory Chair)

Fig. 5-9. Contemporary Lounge Chair, Reversible
T Cushion (Masland)

Types of Joints

The type of joints used in the construction of the frame will determine to a great extent the life of the furniture piece. Some authorities believe the mortise and tenon joint is the only good one for joining one part of a frame to another; others, place great faith in the double-doweled joint. In any case, either type when properly made will outlast all other methods.

Mortise and Tenon Joint

This joint is made by cutting a hole in one member (the mortise) and cutting down the size of the other member (tenon) to fit the mortise. The depth of the mortise should be somewhat greater than the length of the tenon

Fig. 5-10. Queen Anne Wing Chair with Reversible T Cushion (Hickory Chair)

Fig. 5-12. Bertha Keener Gossip Seat (Victorian Furniture)

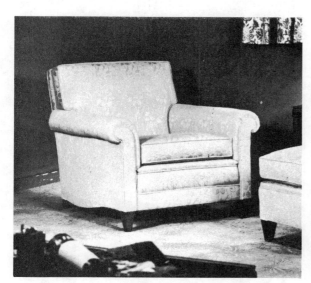

Fig. 5-11. Lawson Chair with Rolled Arms (Berkeley)

Fig. 5-13. Love Seat (Victorian Furniture)

to allow for excess glue and to permit the shoulder of the tenon to fit tightly against the other part of the frame.

Dowel Joint

Such a joint is made by boring holes in each of the frame members to be joined and inserting a piece of dowel rod slightly shorter than the total depth of the holes. Both holes and dowels are brushed with glue. The dowels must be made of well seasoned wood to avoid shrinkage which would cause the joint to become loose. The best dowels for furniture construction have grooves, spiral or longitudinal, cut into them. These grooves provide space for glue thereby increasing holding power. They also permit air to escape, making it easier to drive the dowels into the holes. Double-dowel construction simply employs two dowels at each joint. This is preferred over the use of a single dowel as it increases the holding power and prevents any twisting that might loosen the joint. Frequently in poorly constructed furniture, the joints are merely nailed together with

perhaps a dab of glue added to hold the parts in place. Poor quality glues which become brittle when dry may also be employed in the manufacture of this type of furniture. Frame construction of this kind is the most expensive in the long run for it means early repairs or in many cases complete replacement.

Corner Blocks

All well constructed furniture frames will have corner blocks to reinforce the corners of the seat rails as shown in Fig. 5-14. They are usually 3 or 4 inches long and about 2 or 2½ inches wide and 13/16 of an inch thick. To be most effective they should be well fitted having been cut at the proper angles, glued with a good grade glue, and held in position with wood screws. Hide glue is usually used and is kept at a constant working temperature in a thermostatically controlled electric glue pot and applied with a stiff glue brush. See Fig. 5-15. If corner blocks are used in cheaper grades of furniture, they are frequently poorly fitted and may be only glued or glued and nailed.

Fig. 5-14. Well-Fitted Corner Block (Berkeley)

Fig. 5-15. Applying Glue to Corner Block (Berkeley)

Supplementary Tack Rails

After a piece of overstuffed furniture has been re-upholstered once or twice, the tack rails for the seat of the frame may be in poor condition. If there are not very many old tack holes they may be filled with plastic wood. However, if there are too many holes, supplementary tack rails should be added. These are strips of wood attached to the inside of the seat rails. They may be made of gumwood, poplar, or soft maple that is straight-grained, kiln-dried, and free of knots. The new rails need not be the same width as the old ones, but they should be at least 3 inches in width and 13/16 inch in thickness. They are cut to the inside measurements of the old rails and attached with glue and screws flush with the bottom of the old rails. The screws should be staggered to prevent splitting the old rails.

Streamlining Old Frames

Many of the earlier contemporary pieces of upholstered furniture tended to be large and bulky. This was due to extensive use of pillow springs in arms and the inclusion of a large quantity of stuffing materials in order to build comfort into the furniture. The later use of stuffing materials with greater resiliency such as foam rubber, rubberized hair, and moss eliminated the need for such great bulk. Therefore, many of the old frames can be cut down in size and given smarter, trimmer lines making them more attractive and easier for the housewife to handle when cleaning. This is especially true of the arms of chairs and sofas and sometimes the backs of these pieces. Care must be taken, however, not to weaken the construction of the frame by reducing its size.

Frame Preparation

The following sequence will serve as a checklist in the preparation of a frame prior to re-upholstering:

1. Remove all remaining tacks using a ripping tool and mallet.
2. Sand or plane all splinters caused by tack removal.
3. Fill old tack holes, any large holes, and open knotholes with plastic wood.
4. Install supplementary tack rails if old rails are in poor condition.
5. Use screws and dowels to strengthen any joints which were previously nailed.
6. Check all butt joints and reglue if necessary, replacing any nails with screws.
7. Replace corner blocks or add them where necessary. New corner blocks should be installed with hot hide glue or cold waterproof glue and wood screws. Care should be exercised not to loosen glued joints in the frame when installing the corner blocks. To prevent this, use bar clamps across the frame near the corner.
8. Glue and clamp any cracks in the frame members which might weaken the frame.
9. Finally, refinish any exposed wood such as legs. This should be done before the final covering is applied to avoid soiling and damaging it.

The Stripping Process 6

Stripping is the process of removing the old upholstery material from the piece of furniture by knocking out the old tacks. See Fig. 6-1. It is one of the simplest operations in upholstery and is usually performed in the trade by a beginning apprentice. Even though it is not a difficult operation, certain definite precautions must be followed in order to prevent damage to the frame or to the finish on any exposed parts.

Fig. 6-1. Stripping with Ripping Tool

Using the Ripping Tool

A ripping tool and a mallet are used in stripping. The edge of the ripping tool is placed against the head of the tack and the handle is hit sharply with the mallet. As the blow is struck, a prying motion is applied with the wrist to aid in lifting the tack. This slight motion makes the job easier and speeds up the work. Once this action becomes automatic, the efficiency of the worker is increased. Beginners sometimes substitute a claw tool for the ripping tool because placing the slot in this tool against the tack head helps to prevent slipping. Experienced workers, however, prefer the plain edge of a ripping tool because tacks cannot clog the tool.

In most instances the ripping tool should be held on the frame piece in line with the grain of the wood. This prevents the wood from splitting or opening up. Such damage would decrease the wood's holding power when the new tacks are driven or, in extreme cases, make the piece unusable. To protect any finished surfaces, always drive the ripping tool away from them rather than toward them. Sometimes it may be necessary to drive toward surfaces or against the grain. In these instances tap very lightly with the mallet.

Steps in the Stripping Process

To perform the stripping process, the piece of furniture is first turned upside down on the trestles with the top of the back resting on one trestle and the front edge of the arms resting on the other. Sofas are inverted similarly, with the top of the arm and the back resting on one trestle and the other end on a second trestle. Remove the cambric on the bottom to expose the tacked portions of the outside covers which are attached to the bottom of the frame rails. The old tacks are removed from all four rails.

The piece of furniture is now turned right side up and measurements are made to deter-mine the amount of fabric that will be required. (See Chapter XII, Laying Out the Fabric.) If the design of the chair or sofa is to be changed to the extent that it would affect the size of the fabric pieces, the measurements should be taken after the stuffing is placed and covered with muslin.

After all the measurements are taken and recorded, the remainder of the chair is stripped down to the bare frame. The beginner should be careful to observe the order in which the pieces of fabric were previously attached and the upholstery methods which were employed. This will help him when it comes time to replace each piece of fabric. Be sure to notice which pieces overlap others, the direction and location of pleats, the location of welting, the placement of tacks, etc.

chapter

Refinishing Wood Surfaces

7

The condition of the finish on the exposed parts of the furniture frame should determine the procedure for refinishing. If the finish is scratched, peeled, or badly marked, a complete refinishing job may be needed.

Moderately Damaged Surfaces

For wood surfaces that are not badly marred, the following steps should be taken:

1. Wash and sand surface. Wash with a solution of ½ pound washing soda to 1 gallon warm water. Allow it to dry, and then sand with 280 or 320 finishing abrasive paper.
2. Touch up or restore the color to any off-color portion. Color can be restored by using spirit stain, non-grain-raising stain, or one of the various commercial edge stains.
3. Repair small dents and scratches with "stick" shellac or furniture cement. If damage is slight, it can be built up with varnish or lacquer, depending upon the final finish.

Badly Damaged Surfaces

For badly damaged surfaces that have been previously treated with paint or stain, follow this procedure:

Removing Old Finish

A paint remover is suitable for this. Be sure to shake the liquid well, as the remover is composed of solvents and wax. The wax prevents the solvents from evaporating too rapidly. Use an old brush to apply the remover, since it will loosen the bristles. Apply the remover with a loaded brush and do not brush over the remover. To do so will remove the wax, causing the solvent to evaporate before it has loosened the old finish. Allow the coated surface to remain undisturbed for about 10 minutes.

If the finish is being removed from a flat surface, remove the softened finish with a flat scraper, then rub it down with coarse steel wool. On turned and carved pieces, clean with crumpled paper or burlap and then rub with fine steel wool. Carvings may be cleaned by dipping an old toothbrush into the remover and rubbing the softened finish.

If the old finish does not come off completely, apply the remover again. After the old finish has been completely removed, wash the surface thoroughly with benzine or naphtha and again rub it down, this time with fine steel wool.

Sanding

After removing the old finish and washing, remove the finer hairlike threads which have risen on the grain by using 3/0 garnet paper. Fine steel wool may be used for rubbing curved surfaces.

Bleaching

If the surface is spotty, it will be necessary to bleach the wood. Stain will not cover a spotty surface so that it will appear uniform. The most satisfactory bleaches are the commercial two-solution bleaches. Any leftover bleach must be discarded. An old but clean brush should be used to apply the solution. Allow the bleach to remain until it dries; then wash with alcohol, or a solution of borax in ½ gallon of hot water. Since this operation raises the grain, it is necessary to sandpaper or steel wool the surface. *Note of caution:* Bleaches are poisonous, and *extreme* care should be taken with their use.

Staining

To be sure of a clean surface, brush on a light coat of lacquer thinner. If the thinner does not evaporate quickly and evenly or if spots remain, the indication is that the pores have not been thoroughly cleaned. In that event, wash the surface down with thinner and retest.

Apply the stain with a clean brush. Spread it evenly; then with a soft cloth, free of lint, wipe the stain evenly with the grain. Do not leave streaks or spots of stain on the surface. Allow this to dry for at least 12 hours. If an oil stain is used, allow at least overnight for drying and more if necessary.

Applying Filler

Filler is used to fill the pores of the wood. Open-grained woods — ash, chestnut, mahogany, oak, and walnut — are filled with a paste wood filler. The close-grained woods — maple, beech, birch, fir, spruce, and pine — may receive a liquid filler.

First apply a coat of thin shellac, 4 parts alcohol and 1 part shellac or sealer. Observe the drying time, and then sand the surface lightly and dust well before filling. Thin the filler with benzene, naphtha, or turpentine to the consistency of thick paint. Do not use a wood-distilled turpentine for thinning or cleaning, since it leaves a greasy film which prevents the lacquer from drying. Tint the filler to approximate the color of the stain, using oil colors. Apply the filler with an old, stubby, rather stiff brush, not so stiff as to scratch the surface, however. Apply freely by brushing lengthwise first, than across the grain to insure penetration of the material deep into the pores of the wood. The filler is ready to be wiped only when it begins to dull or set. To rub off the filler use rags that will not leave lint on the surface, such as burlap, jute, or sea grass. Rub across the grain first, then with the grain lightly. Allow 24-48 hours drying time.

Applying Varnish

If the surface is to be varnished, see that the area in which the work is being done is free from dust. Apply with a clean brush, being sure to remove all loose bristles and dust. Brush the varnish on with a full brush, first across the grain; then blend it in long straight strokes with the grain. Do not go over the work once the varnish has begun to set. On vertical surfaces, be sure to check for runs or sags. In wiping down runs with the brush, do not have the brush loaded with varnish. The work should dry at least overnight at room temperature.

Before applying a second coat, sand the surface lightly with 3/0 sandpaper, being sure to sand with the grain. Dust the work thoroughly. Apply the second coat as you did the first, allowing it to dry 48 hours. Then rub the surface with pumice stone and oil, or pumice and water. Oil will result in a dull, satin finish, whereas water will result in a fine, bright finish.

When the work has been rubbed, it must be cleaned. If water has been used, the surface must be cleaned with a dampened cloth and then waxed. If oil has been used, clean with benzene or naphtha and a soft cloth. To obtain a finer finish, rub with rottenstone after allowing 12-15 hours for drying after the previous treatment. Finish off by cleaning and then applying wax and polish.

Attaching Webbing 8

Webbing is the strong, closely woven material made from jute which is used to support the springs. It is superior to most of the sag-proof types of construction because it provides greater resiliency. Its use fell into ill repute during the great depression of the thirties, but this was due to the inferior grades of webbing made, the use of cheap materials for frames, and improper methods of tacking it. When webbing continually kept breaking and the bottoms of chairs and couches sagged to the floor, people became suspicious of its value as a practical means of supporting springs. Metal straps and heavy wire were substituted and many people were convinced that this was the answer to the problem. The result, however, was less comfortable furniture. When a good grade of webbing is properly applied on a good frame, it gives the most satisfactory results, with the possible exception of the more expensive spring suspension construction. See Fig. 8-1.

Selecting Webbing

Webbing is manufactured in three different grades and widths. (See "Jute Webbing" in Chapter III.) The widest width and the best

quality (red striped) should be used to support the seat springs. It is false economy to use an inferior grade of webbing for this part of a chair as the greatest strain occurs here.

Application Procedure

In attaching webbing, fold the first end back about one inch and place it on the frame with

Fig. 8-1. Bottom View of Chair Showing Webbing and Twine Holding Springs

71

the folded part out. This provides a layer of webbing between the tack heads and the strip of webbing which will support the springs thus preventing the tack from cutting the webbing. Seven tacks are used to hold the end of the webbing. They are staggered to prevent splitting the frame. Toeing the tacks slightly will

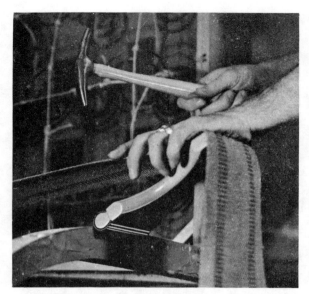

Fig. 8-2. First Position of Webbing Stretcher in Applying Webbing

Fig. 8-3. Tacking Webbing in Position after Being Stretched

give them greater holding power. Use No. 10 or 12 tacks, depending upon the hardness of the wood. The longest tacks which can be driven without splitting the frame should be used.

The second end of the strip of webbing is attached by using a webbing stretcher. The stretcher is placed in position at about a 30 degree angle, and then forced down into a horizontal position. See Figs. 8-2 and 8-3. If the strand of webbing is not tight enough, the stretcher may be forced further down. A stretcher with a rounded end covered with rubber works well, as the rubber prevents the tool from slipping. The webbing should be stretched as taut as possible without unduly springing the frame. When the webbing is stretched the proper amount, three tacks are driven to hold it, one in the center and the other two spaced in from the edge a distance of about one-fourth the width of the webbing. The stretcher is then removed, and the webbing is cut about one inch beyond the frame and folded back over the three tacks. Four more tacks are then driven through the folded piece. They should be staggered in reference to the first three tacks to prevent splitting the frame. Care

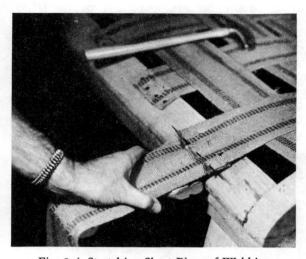

Fig. 8-4. Stretching Short Piece of Webbing

should be taken to space the webbing equally and to lay it parallel to the frame.

A strip of webbing is placed under each row of springs and interwoven to give greater strength. To eliminate waste, a piece at the end of a roll which is long enough to go across the frame but too short to use the stretcher may be joined to another strip by weaving a regulator or heavy needle through them so that the stretcher may then be used as illustrated in Fig. 8-4.

To save time an upholsterer attaches several beginning ends at the same time, working from both ends of a roll of webbing and sometimes from two or three rolls at a time. He then stretches them one after another, driving three tacks in each, cuts them all and folds back each one and tacks it. A beginner can save considerable time by applying two strips at a time by working from both ends of the roll.

Sewing and Tying Springs

9

The first step in attaching springs is sewing them to the webbing using sewing twine. They are then tied to the frame using spring twine. Once tied, they are covered with burlap and sewed to this. Fig. 9-2 explains the operations

Fig. 9-1. Sewing Spring to Webbing Using Double Pointed Needle

followed in sewing the springs to the webbing and burlap.

Sewing Springs to Webbing

A straight, double-pointed needle is used to sew the springs to the webbing. It is easier to start with an end spring of the back row. The spring is placed in the desired location; the needle is passed up from the underside of the webbing near the bottom coil of the spring, then down on the opposite side of the spring coil; this loops the twine around the coil. See Fig. 9-1. A knot is tied at the end of the twine, and a slip knot is used to secure the first loop around the spring. The needle is passed up and down to form loops at four points on the spring. The first and last loops on each spring are knotted so that each spring is secured individually. Thus, if the twine should break, only one spring could shift. The twine passes from one loop to the other along the underneath side of the webbing forming the letter "U" under each spring. On the last spring of each row, the four loops are sewn in a sequence which will bring the last stitch adjacent to the next spring to be sewn.

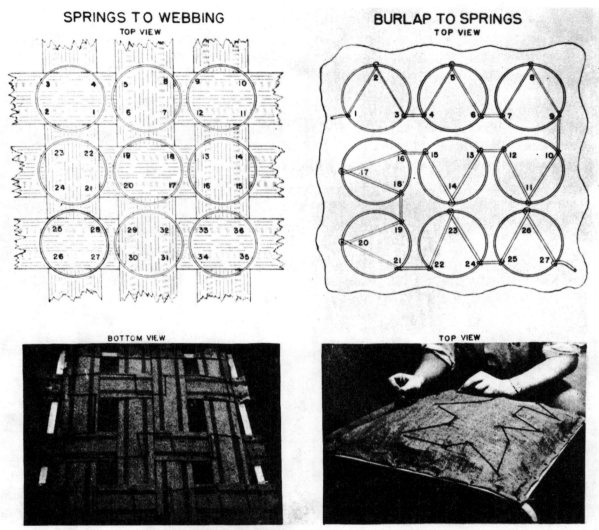

Fig. 9-2. Sewing Springs to Webbing and Burlap (Schramm)

Fastening Springs to Frame

After the springs are sewed to the webbing in the proper location, the tops of the springs are tied to the frame with spring twine. A piece of twine is cut for each row of springs; its length should be about three times the distance across the frame. Two No. 12 tacks are driven into the frame on each side of a center line for the row of springs. These should be about one-half inch apart and driven only half way. A loop made in the twine (about a foot from one end), is placed between the two tacks.

Then it is taken back over the heads of the tacks and drawn tight. See Fig. 9-3. The tacks are then driven all the way into the wood. The loop around the tacks prevents the main strand from rubbing against the sharp edge of the tack heads and being cut.

The long end of the twine is then secured to the spring with a clove hitch as illustrated in Figs. 9-4 and 9-5. It is best to use a clove hitch on all ties. Some upholsterers use a clove hitch on one side of the spring and a half hitch on the other side, but this is not as effective.

If a box shape is desired the first clove hitch is placed on the second or third coil on the opposite side of the spring.

When the last clove hitch is made on the last spring in the row, two No. 12 tacks are driven half way into the frame. The twine is drawn between them, looped around one and passed behind the other to keep it from slipping. One hand is used to pull the spring: the

fingers are hooked around the spring coil where the last clove hitch was made and the thumb is braced against the outside of the frame. The

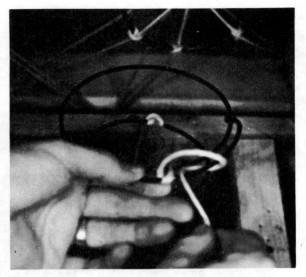

Fig. 9-5. Second Loop of Clove Hitch

Fig. 9-3. Attaching First End of Spring Twine
to Tack Rail

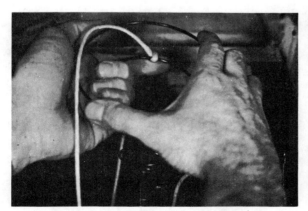

Fig. 9-4. Start of Clove Hitch for a Box Shape

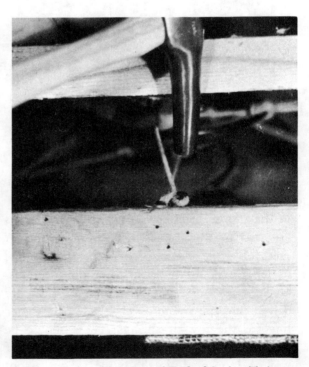

Fig. 9-6. Attaching Second End of Spring Twine
to Tack Rail

other hand is used to loop the twine around the first tack and behind the second. The hand gripping the spring is then shifted to hold the end of the twine thus freeing the other hand to use the hammer. The first tack (which has the loop around it) is driven all the way into the frame. See Fig. 9-6. This will hold the strain while the loop is placed around the second tack which is then driven into the frame. Both ends that are left are then tied first to one side of the top coil of the spring with a clove hitch and then to the opposite side. These ends are known in the trade as the "tie backs." The same procedure is followed for each row of springs.

Each spring should be tied at right angles and diagonally in two directions providing eight clove hitches on each spring. When the last diagonal is being tied on each row, a clove hitch is made at the center of each spring where the cords cross.

Covering with Burlap

After the springs are tied to the frame a piece of burlap is tacked to the frame to cover the springs and prevent the stuffing from going down between them. The edges of the burlap are folded back to give a double thickness under the tack heads. The piece should be drawn snugly but not so tightly that it would take the strain off the spring cords, as this might cause the burlap to break after short usage. After the burlap has been tacked in position, each spring is sewed to the burlap. Sewing twine and a curved needle are used and three stitches are made on each spring. The first and last stitch should be knotted as when sewing the springs to the webbing.

Materials for Stuffing 10

Great care must be exercised in the preparation, positioning, and anchoring of the stuffing materials because the success of the final upholstering depends so much on these operations. The comfort, appearance, and durability of the finished piece of furniture is dependent to a great extent not only upon the type and amount of stuffing material used, but also upon the methods of positioning, regulating, and anchoring it so that it will remain in the desired position even under hard usage.

Common Materials and Their Uses

The common types of stuffing materials include tow, moss, palm fiber, hair, sisal, and cotton.

Tow

This is a flax straw grown in the Great Lakes region of the United States and Canada. It is purchased by the pound and in 100-pound bales. It is used for making firm solid bases or foundations, chiefly on seats and the tops of arms. Since it is packed very compactly for shipping, it has to be loosened up and pulled

apart by hand or with a mechanical fiber picker. A liberal amount of tow should be used as it will repack when it is sewed or drawn in position with burlap. Formerly it was used in making spring edges for seats, but today the arduous task of sewing spring and roll edges by hand has practically been replaced by the use of spring edging and roll edging, Fig. 10-1. For seat foundations the tow is positioned uniformly on top of the burlap spring covering and sewed securely to it with a curved needle and stitching twine. On the top of arms, the

Fig. 10-1. Spring and Roll Edgings
(Schramm at Northwest)

tow is distributed uniformly on the top of the frame. Then a layer of burlap is tacked on one edge of the arm frame, drawn over the tow tightly and tacked on the other edge of the arm frame. Sometimes the shredded leaves of palm trees, called *palm fiber,* are substituted for tow.

Sisal

This coarse fibrous plant grown in the tropics is used as an inexpensive stuffing in place of tow. Frequently sisal is rubberized and made into pads as foundations for seats, backs, and for use over arms and spring units in cushions, Fig. 10-2. Hogs' hair is also rubberized and used in the same manner. Another substitute for tow is *coconut fiber.* It is obtained from the coarse, short, curly fibers of the outer husk of coconuts. Although it is not very resilient, it does give a firm foundation.

Moss

Spanish moss is a vine which grows in the trees in the swampy areas of the Gulf states of Louisiana, Mississippi, Alabama, and Florida. When dried, it is very resilient and can be purchased by the pound or in 100-pound bales. Before being used it must be pulled apart by hand or with a fiber picker similar to tow. However, since moss grows up in trees and is picked with long hooked poles, many twigs and small dead branches are picked with the moss. Extreme care must be exercised to remove all small twigs as these could work to the surface and puncture the covering material. The moss is positioned evenly and then sewed to the burlap with hemp stitching twine and a curved needle, Fig. 10-3. Some upholsterers sew and tie loops of twine in place first and then tuck the moss through the loops. Although this does a better job of anchoring, a beginner can do a satisfactory job just by sewing it tightly and tying a knot after every stitch or two. Regard-

less of the method of anchoring use a liberal amount of stuffing material as it will compress when the muslin and covering material are pulled in position and tacked. The tendency for beginners is to understuff, not overstuff.

Hogs' Hair

Curled hogs' hair is a fine, resilient stuffing material frequently used in place of moss. Curled hair can be purchased by the pound or in 50-pound burlap bags. Sometimes it is used in combination with moss, with a layer of curled hair placed on top of the moss to give a softer, smoother surface. However, since moths are attracted to animal fibers, hogs' hair should be mothproofed. Sometimes the hogs' hair is rubberized to give it even greater resiliency and to aid in mothproofing. Rubberized

Fig. 10-2. Sisal Pad (Upholstery Supply)

Fig. 10-3. Positioning Moss

Fig. 10-4. Sewing Rubberized Curled Hair
Seat Foundation in Position (Armour)

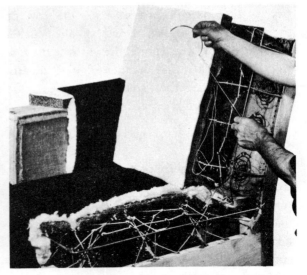

Fig. 10-6. Sewing Rubberized Hair Foundation
to Springs (Armour)

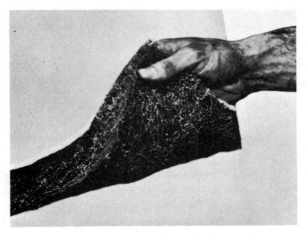

Fig. 10-5. Rubberized Hair Foundation with
Top Layer of Foam Rubber (Armour)

Cotton is usually a blend of different types of cotton fibers. Texas cotton is somewhat harsh and rough, but it gives a blend good body. Virginia cotton is soft and fluffy and gives a blend the quality of softness. Its fibers are short, however, and it would not work well by itself as it would not stay together. Imported Egyptian cotton used in a blend helps the cotton to stay together since its fibers are long. When using rolls never cut the cotton with shears as this is not only difficult but would leave an abrupt edge. Rather pull it apart by hand to give it a gradually tapered feather edge.

hair is also matted to form foundations as seen in Fig. 10-4. It may have a top layer of foam rubber joined to it for greater comfort, Fig. 10-5. Its actual positioning is shown in Fig. 10-6.

Cotton Batting

This stuffing material is used as the top layer on all parts of overstuffed furniture including cushions. It may be purchased by the pound in 15-pound rolls or in 100-pound bales.

Other Materials

Additional stuffing materials used chiefly in soft cushions and pillow type chairs include: down, obtained from the undercoating of ducks and geese; mixtures of feathers and down from ducks and geese; goose or chicken feathers (separate or mixed); and kapok, processed from the silky fibers of the silk-cotton or kapok tree. All of these cushion stuffings may be purchased by the pound or in one- or five-pound bags or in 100-pound bales.

chapter 11

Selecting Upholstering Fabrics

A wide variety of textile fabrics may be used for covering overstuffed furniture. The fabric selected should complement its surroundings. If the piece is to be used in a setting with period furniture, figured tapestries are quite appropriate; if it is to be placed in the same room with modern furniture, plain fabrics with a subdued pattern are more suitable; however, if the particular piece of furniture is an antique, a fabric similar to what was used originally would be best. For example, an antique velvet tapestry, needlepoint, or a horsehair fabric might be selected.

Color

The choice of color is another important consideration. Light solid colors or material which contrasts with the wall will make furniture look larger. Figured designs with a background that harmonizes with the color of the walls will make a piece of furniture seem smaller. Warm colors — such as reds, yellows, oranges, red-violets, browns, sands, pinks, roses, rusts, and wines — are stimulating colors which tend to advance and make furniture covered with them appear larger. Cool colors — such as blues, greens, blue-violets, and their various shades — are restful colors which are said to recede and make furniture covered with them seem smaller. Greys and charcoals are neutral and may be used alone or with all colors.

The size of the design of a fabric should be considered in relation to the size of the piece of furniture to be covered. Large individual patterns or designs should be reserved for large pieces of furniture. Small pieces of furniture look best when a small figured pattern or an overall pattern is used.

If upholstery is to have hard usage, inconspicuous patterns and colors that will not show soil should be chosen. A few silk, rayon, or metal threads shot through the cotton, wool, or hair upholstery fabric give it luster and additional beauty.

Usage

The conditions under which the furniture will be used should also be considered in the selection of cover fabrics. In homes where there are many young children it is wise to select a strong, durable fabric such as a mohair, nylon, or wool. These sturdy fibers are able to withstand friction and dry cleaning. For durability, yarns should be tightly twisted and closely woven. In homes having pets the use of fabrics having a loop pile or raised threads should be avoided as they are easily snagged and will look shabby in a short time. Where there are no young children, the more decorative fabrics such as silk and rayon may be used to advantage.

Cost

Another important consideration in the selection of upholstery fabrics is the cost to the person for whom the piece of furniture is being covered. If the person is financially able to re-cover the furniture frequently, he will have a wider range of selection; however, if he must be prudent, he needs to select fabric with durability in mind. It is not always wise to select the cheapest fabric available as it might wear out quickly. A relatively new process is now being used which coats the reverse side of the fabric with a rubberized substance. This helps to prevent stretching and threads from pulling, and gives the fabric more body. At only a slight increase in cost it greatly improves the wearing quality of the material.

Slipcovers

Upholstery fabric retains its freshness longer if it is covered during the summer months. Linen and cotton fabrics are excellent for summer use as slipcovers; they make a chair or sofa upholstered in wool seem cooler. A formal room can be changed into an informal one with bright, cheerful designs in chintz or cretonne. If upholstery is somewhat shabby, new slipcovers will freshen it. Some of the fabrics commonly used for slipcovers are chintz, cretonne, linen, crash, cotton rep, and denim.

Care of Upholstery

Upholstered furniture should be brushed and vacuum cleaned frequently, not only to remove dirt, but to prevent moths from attacking wool. When a new piece of furniture is bought, make sure the upholstery material is treated chemically to make it mothproof. A muslin covering inside the upholstery fabric will keep moths from the inside of the furniture.

Spots should be removed when they first appear, with either soap and water (if fabric is washable) or a dry cleaning fluid. A white fabric can often be cleaned at home by sprinkling it with dry powdered magnesia and then brushing it off. If upholstery is badly soiled, take it to a reliable upholsterer or cleaning specialist for cleaning.

Kinds of Upholstery Fabrics

Some of the most commonly used fabrics for upholstered furniture and cushions are frieze (in wool, mohair, or cotton), brocade, damask, brocatelle, plush, nylon, velvet, velour, mohair, haircloth, tapestry, plastic, leather, and leather substitutes.

Armure (French)

The name given to small ridgy patterns like bird's eye, pebble, diamond, or pattern similar to chain armour; a twilled fabric of silk, wool, cotton, rayon, or mixture.

Artificial Leather

Trade name is "leather cloth"; a cotton fabric (sateen, drill, or duck) which is coated with a pyroxylin solution and has a leather grain stamped on the surface; washable, scrub proof, and wear resistant; colors do not fade from effects of time, sun, or the elements; a most economical material for fine upholstery. It is 50 inches wide and a roll contains 50 to 60 yards.

Bengaline

Similar to ordinary rep or poplin with cords extending lengthwise or crosswise; made of cotton, wool, silk, or rayon; an imitation of an old silk fabric made for many centuries in Bengal, India.

Brocade

Luxurious, silk fabric in Jacquard weave with figures, flowers, foliage, or other ornament in a raised pattern; often enriched with gold or silver metal threads; not reversible as damask is; comes in a mixture of fibers so that most Jacquard figured goods of fair quality are now called brocade.

Brocatelle

Similar to brocade but heavier; designs are raised with Jacquard weave; comes in mixture of cotton, silk, or rayon fibers.

Broché

French word for "swivel"; fabric made in either swivel or lappet weave of silk; raised pattern is not part of fabric itself; ground is satin or taffeta with striped or all over figures.

Burlap

Plain cloth woven from jute or hemp; a coarse, stiff material used for covering springs in upholstery work; grades are commonly known as 8 oz. or light, 10 oz. or medium, 12 oz. or heavy; standard width is 40 inches; however, it is obtainable in 36-inch and 45-inch widths.

Cambric

A medium-weight muslin with a slightly glazed or polished surface produced by calendering; it is either black or white; white cambric is used for cushion and pillow casing; black cambric is used for tacking underneath upholstered furniture; first made in Cambric, France.

Chintz

Cotton fabric like cretonne with a pattern of many colors; the glazed finish prevents dust and dirt from adhering readily; chintz is the Hindu word meaning variegated.

Corduroy

Sturdy cotton fabric having a cut pile and a ribbed surface; the cords or ribs run lengthwise of the material; name is derived from the French, "corde du roi", meaning a king's cord.

Crash

Rather heavy fabric made of irregular tow yarns in plain weave; may be hand-blocked, printed, or embroidered.

Cretonne

A lightweight cloth of cotton or linen, in a plain weave with a printed pattern; closely woven and much heavier than muslin; it is the lightest in weight of upholstery coverings; originated in Norman village of Creton in northwest France.

Damask

Made of cotton, wool, silk, rayon, or a combination of these; background is bright and glossy with flowers, vines, and figures in a contrasting Jacquard weave; pattern is woven so that the figures are reversed on the wrong side; name was first applied to fabric made in Damascus; used for upholstery of very fine furniture.

Denim

A strong, twilled cotton fabric of superior wearing qualities; usually plain colored, though a small pattern may be woven into it; plain denim is used for upholstering under seat cushions; figured denim is used for upholstering furniture; denim is usually 36 inches wide.

Faille

A cotton, rayon, or silk fabric in rib variations of plain weave; ribs run fillingwise and are not so large as grossgrain; similar to poplin or rep.

Friezé

Looped, springy, pile fabric of cotton, wool, or rayon; pile is uncut; has crosswise rows of small looped pile. This type of fabric is known as bouclé.

Haircloth or Horsehair

A stiff, wiry fabric of cotton warp with a filling of hair from the horse's mane. The hair is so interwoven that the filling threads bend over the warp and form the wearing surface. The cloth is woven as wide as the length of the hair, usually from 20 to 24 inches. It was formerly made only in plain black, but at present it can be obtained in several plain colors, with a number of intricate patterns. Being a narrow cloth with a small pattern, it is used on small occasional chairs and dining room chairs.

Leather

Cowhides used for upholstery leathers, are split into from three to five thicknesses. Leather is sold to the upholstery trade by the hide or square foot. It is obtainable in different colors.

Matelessé

A cotton, rayon, or silk fabric having raised patterns which are usually of one color with a rich flowered design which shows only by its relief or embossed appearance.

Mohair

Made from hair of the Angora goat; mohair is woven into a cotton or wool background. One of the chief advantages of mohair, compared with other fabrics, is that its natural luster is not destroyed nor dulled during the many processes of manufacture; it excels in durability, hence it is used on articles subjected to hard wear; its only disadvantage is that being an animal fiber it is subject to moths. The pile is woven in loops; for plain mohair, the loops are cut after weaving, so that the pile stands upright. If the pile is left uncut, the fabric is called "mohair frieze". A brocade effect is obtained by shearing or burning the pile to form a background lower than the design. The thickness of the goods varies according to the height of the pile, and the quality according to the firmness of weave and the quality of mohair yarns used in the pile; an imitation mohair is manufactured commercially of rayon and cotton and is cheaper in price.

Moire

Finely ribbed silk or rayon fabric with a watered design; a fragile, dressy fabric.

Muslin

A lightweight, open-textured cotton cloth of plain weave, originally made in Mosul, the ancient city of Mesopotamia; many varieties of muslin are sold under such names as batiste, lawn, nainsook, etc., due to difference in construction, quality of yarn, and kind of finish; muslin is sold bleached or unbleached; heavy, wide unbleached muslin is used for the inner or first covering, especially on custom-made pieces of furniture.

Nylon

A synthetic fiber developed by the Du Pont Company which is woven into a sleek, closely textured fabric in plain colors; it is extremely durable and long wearing; it is rather expensive in price and is often used in a mixture with other fibers.

Plastics

Synthetic fabric resembling leather; it has a slick, somewhat shiny surface which excels in wearing qualities because it resists scuffing, cracking, peeling, sunlight, and stains of all kinds; sold commercially under various trade names, as Duran, Boltaflex, and Fabrilite; Boltaflex is manufactured in multi-color prints as well as plain colors; Du Pont "Fabrilite" is made of vinyl plastic. Plastic coverings may be solid, on a textile base, or on a stretch fabric backing.

Plush

Very heavy fabric in pile weave; pile is longer than that of velvet or velour; inexpensive; used on cheaper grades of furniture; cotton, silk, or rayon.

Rep and Poplin

Similar types of transversely ribbed fabrics; rep is a little heavier than poplin; produced from cotton in a wide range of weights and constructions which vary from heavy Jacquard-figured or plain upholstery covering to lightweight shirting; rep also comes in wool.

Sateen

Soft fabric woven in sateen weave; lustrous surface may be plain or printed; plain colors are suitable for lining draperies; "Glosheen," a type of heavy sateen having multi-colored flower prints or plain colors, is used for upholstering boudoir chairs or chaise lounges. The surface is somewhat sleek in appearance but not glazed as chintz is; its chief use is for drapery and slipcover material; made from cotton.

Satin

Lustrous cloth in warp satin weave; made from silk, cotton, or rayon; a very dressy fabric used on fine furniture.

Taffeta

Very crisp, dull fabric in plain weave; many taffetas are weighted to produce crispness, called scroop; excessive weighting causes fabric to crack; some taffetas have slight fillingwise ribs; some are quilted or embroidered; made of silk or rayon; rayon taffeta does not have crispness of silk taffeta and is unweighted.

Tapestry

Heavy fabric made of wool, silk, cotton, linen, or a combination of these; handmade tapestry usually has a pictorial design; machine-made tapestries have elaborate Jacquard designs in varied colors which are an imitation of those made by hand; their colors are not so beautiful, nor are the patterns so carefully worked out. It is a most durable decorative fabric and varies in price according to the composition, size, and design. It will not ravel, and dust and moths find difficulty destroying it.

Toile de Jouy

Printed cotton originated by Oberkampf in France at the time of Louis XVI; printed scenes represent life of the times; used as a drapery or slipcover material and often to upholster French Provincial furniture.

Tweed

Heavy fabric made in hand-woven effects of wool, cotton, or in combination with rayon.

Velvet

Luxurious fabric in pile weave made of cotton, silk, linen, or a mixture of these materials; lighter than velour; pile may be pressed one way or may stand erect; may have a silk pile and cotton back; fabric may be treated to give an antique appearance; pile may be cut to give a flowered relief which is termed Jacquard velvet; used on fine furniture.

Velveteen

All cotton, short pile fabric imitating silk velvet; may be woven in colors and patterns; a closely woven, sturdy fabric originally called fustian; the soft mercerized cotton filling yarns form floats which are later cut and brushed into the short pile; used as an inexpensive imitation of velvet.

Velour (French)

Short, thick, warp pile fabric; made of cotton, silk, linen, or rayon; heavier than velvet.

Venetian

Sturdy, closely woven face yarn in reverse twist; made of cotton highly mercerized to imitate satin; heavier than and superior to sateen.

Laying Out the Fabric 12

In the construction of a new piece of uphol-stered furniture, the required amount of fabric is determined after the muslin covers are attached. In re-upholstering an old piece of furniture, it is advisable to take measurements during the stripping operation. After the out-side covers (back and sides) are removed, it is possible to take accurate measurements for all pieces of fabric which will be needed. Allow-ances should be made for any modifications in the frame design which will affect the size of the fabric pieces.

Recording Measurements

To determine the amount of material needed with a minimum amount of waste, it is desir-able to list in table form the name, number of pieces, and size of each part. These may be numbered consecutively to aid in quick identi-fication on the layout form. The same numbers can also be chalked on the reverse side of the fabric for easy identification.

In measuring the size of each piece of fabric that will be required, it is advisable to measure the width first and then the length. By con-sistently following this order, mistakes of laying out and cutting a piece in the wrong direction will be avoided. A non-stretchable cloth tape, six feet long, such as a sateen tape, or a flexible steel rule is handy for measuring, especially around irregular shapes. On the first few jobs make generous allowances for pulling and tacking the fabric — about two or three inches is generally sufficient. Allow $\frac{1}{2}$ inch for all seams which are to be sewed by machine and at least $1\frac{1}{2}$ inches for the width of welting. This will be sufficient for welting that is $5/32$ of an inch in diameter. Larger diameter welts will require wider strips. Welting is the rolled edge that is used to finish the edges of cushions, to hide seams, or to decorate the intersections of two adjacent parts of a piece of furntiure.

As the measurements are made, make a tabu-lar list of all required pieces. Include the num-ber of pieces, their names, and their sizes as shown in the examples.

First, measure the covers (the outside cover-ing of arms and back), then remove them. This facilitates the easy measurement of the other pieces. The welting should be measured next.

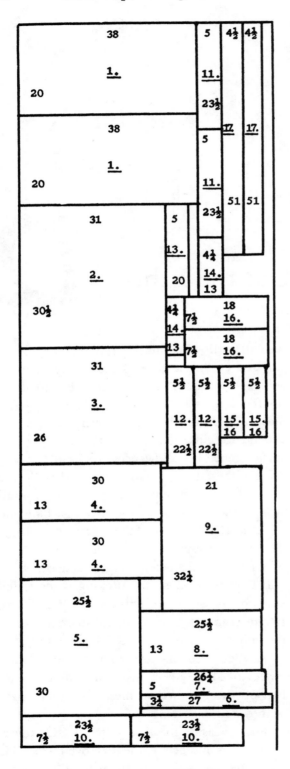

Fig. 12-1. Cutting Layout for a Tilt-Back Lounge Chair with Fixed Cushion and Foot Stool

Add the lengths of all the pieces to find the total amount of welting required and record it on the list. Material for welting is cut either on the bias (diagonally) or along the length of the fabric. In the trade it is usually cut on the bias. Some fabrics make it absolutely necessary to cut the welting in strips along the length of the cloth, as they will not feed into the special sewing machines for making welting if cut diagonally. Continue measuring the rest of the pieces and list their names and sizes. Numbering the parts makes it easy to refer to them on the cutting plan.

Making Layout Plan

Two layout plans are shown as examples in Figs. 12-1 and 12-2. The first involves the pieces for a tilt-back lounge chair with fixed cushion and foot stool, while the second is a plan of the pieces for a three-cushion Lawson sofa. On

Cutting Layout for a Tilt-Back Lounge Chair with Fixed Cushion and Foot Stool

No. of Pieces	Name of Part	Width	Length	Layout No.
2	Side Covers	38	20	1
1	Inside Back	31	30½	2
1	Top of Stool	31	26	3
2	Inside of Arms	30	13	4
1	Back Cover	25½	30	5
1	Rear Top Piece	27	3¼	6
1	Forward Top Piece	26¼	5	7
1	Front	25½	13	8
1	Seat	21	32¼	9
2	Sides of Stool	23½	7½	10
2	Sides of Seat	5	23½	11
2	Forward Sides of the Back	5½	22½	12
1	Seat Back	5	20	13
2	Rear Sides of Back	4¼	13	14
2	Front of Arms	5½	16	15
2	Ends of Stool	18	7½	16
2	Panels	4½	51	17
1	Welting	1½	300	—

Amount of Fabric Needed 4 4/9 yards
Adding the lengths of the pieces on the left side gives 160 inches or 4 4/9 yds.

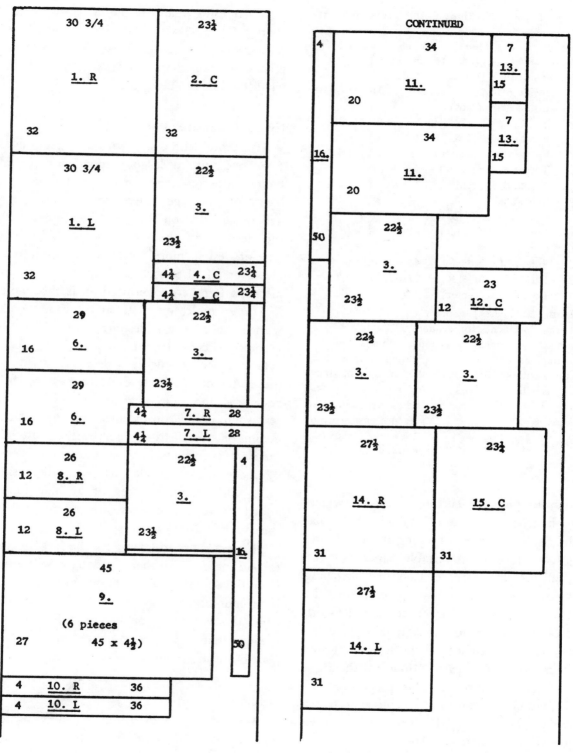

Fig. 12-2. Cutting Layout for a Three-Cushion
Lawson Sofa

Cutting Layout for a Three-Cushion Lawson Sofa

No. of Pieces	Name of Part	Width	Length	Layout No.
2	Inside Back (L & R)	30¾	32	1
1	Inside Back (center)	23¼	32	2
2	Inside Arms	29	16	6
2	Inside Arms (front)	7	15	13
2	End Covers	34	20	11
2	Front of Seat (L & R)	26	12	8
1	Front of Seat (center)	23	12	12
2	Top of Sofa (L & R)	36	4	10
1	Top of Sofa (center)	23¼	4	4
2	Side Panels	4	50	16
2	Front Panels (L & R)	28	4	7
1	Front Panel (center)	23	4	5
6	Cushions	22½	23½	3
6	Sides of Cushions	45	4½	9
2	Back Cover (L & R)	27½	31	14
1	Back Cover (center)	23¼	31	15

Welting   200 inches for sofa
Welting   540 inches for cushions
Denim   2⅓ yards for seat under cushions

Amount of Fabric Needed	
6¾ yards without back cover	Adding lengths along the left side of drawing gives 242 or 304 inches depending on presence or absence of back cover — thus 6¾ or 8½ yards.
8½ yards with back cover	

the layout plan for cutting, draw the widest piece first on the top left-hand side of the diagram. Sketch all pieces keeping the width and length in proportion. Graph paper is quite helpful for this purpose. Continue sketching down the left side of your plan, taking the widest pieces first, until you come to a width that can be placed to the right alongside the last piece you sketched on the lower left side of your diagram. Then continue up the right side. Slight variations in this procedure will sometimes enable you to fit the pieces to better advantage, but in general this method will save a great deal of material. An exception to this procedure is illustrated at the lower right hand side of the sample layout.

When using material 54 inches wide, the chart in Fig. 12-3 will be helpful in determining the amount of material required. A well-planned cutting chart will often result in somewhat less material being needed.

Layout for Spot Pattern

If a fabric with a spot pattern is being used (i.e., one with a large predominant central figure or design), it is necessary to plan the layout of the largest pieces so that the design will be centered on them and be aligned with the designs on the other pieces. With this type of design, more fabric is usually needed. However, if the back and inside arms are pieced, a fairly economical layout is obtainable.

For example, on material 54 inches wide with a spot repeat design every 27 inches (centers of central figure in pattern 27 inches apart) a piece 27 inches wide can be used for the center of the back. Small pieces are then added on the sides near the top where the seams will not be conspicuous. Pulls made from denim or other strong inexpensive materials can be sewed where they will not show. Pieces 27 inches wide are also used for the inside arms with smaller pieces of regular fabric added where it will show and pulls sewed to the ends of the small pieces.

It is necessary in laying out the large pieces to position them so that the designs will align laterally. Some material may be saved by using both ends of your layout for large pieces and using the center for smaller pieces. It is recommended that beginners avoid spot patterns and start out using plain or overall designs.

Adding Welting

After sketching in the major pieces which will be needed, draw strips 1½ inches in width and as long as possible on the bias of the layout. These will be used for welting. Short pieces are

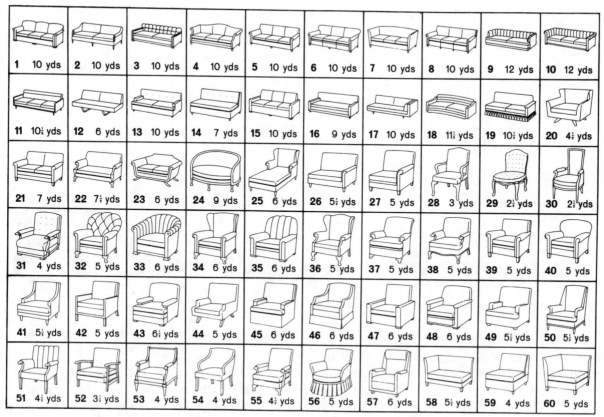

Fig. 12-3. Quick Reference Yardage Chart for 54-Inch Material (U.S. Rubber)

sometimes used to save material, however, the longest pieces possible are preferable as this eliminates unnecessary seams which are somewhat bulky and unsightly. The welting can be joined face to face at the ends to form one continuous strip. This way all the welting that will be needed can be sewed at one time.

The required amount of fabric is computed by adding the lengths of all pieces on the left side of the layout plan. Dividing the total number of inches by thirty-six gives the number of yards required.

Planning the layout of the pieces needed is one of the important steps in upholstering.

Cutting Layout

To lay out the material for cutting, place the fabric on a cutting table with the reverse side up. Following your layout diagram, mark the pieces using a stick of white chalk sharpened to a wedge point. Numbering the piece according to your list avoids mix-ups, especially if you have several pieces nearly alike. All pieces should be laid out before any are cut to be sure that you have sufficient material. After the pieces are cut, stack them, by pairs, face-to-face to prevent chalk from transferring to the face of the fabric. Large pieces can be folded reverse side out to keep them clean.

Applying Covering Materials 13

A beginning upholsterer is often baffled by the trick of applying a piece of fabric without having wrinkles spoil the appearance of the finished job. If the proper procedure is followed, this problem disappears almost immediately.

General Procedure

It is only necessary to start tacking at the centers of the four sides of the piece and to continue tacking toward the corners. The material should be placed in position and *temporary* tacks driven in part way at the centers of each of the four sides. Toeing the tacks toward the direction of pull helps to prevent them from popping out. Draw the material sufficiently tight to give the desired effect. If it is drawn too tightly, the result will be a hard uncomfortable product; if the material is not pulled tightly enough, the fabric will wrinkle and sag after very little use.

Once the first four temporary tacks have been located, start drawing the fabric diagonally toward the side and corner at the same time. Tack near the center first and work to-

ward the corners. Work on two opposite sides at the same time to keep the lines in the fabric straight. When you finish these, tack the other two sides following the same procedure. A little practice is all that is required to produce a professional looking job.

The following hints and suggestions may prove helpful to the beginner in applying covering materials:

Tacking

In tacking covering material, the beginner may find it advantageous to temporary tack (drive tacks halfway), not only the first tacks driven in at the centers of the four sides, but also the remaining edges. If adjustments are needed, these tacks can be easily removed and the fabric cover restretched to the proper position. An experienced upholsterer uses the side of his hammer to knock out temporary tacks, but the beginner may feel safer in using the ripping tool to keep from damaging the fabric. See Fig. 13-1.

In driving tacks through covering materials, the tacks must not be hit after they have been

Fig. 13-1. Removing a Temporary Tack with Mallet and Ripping Tool

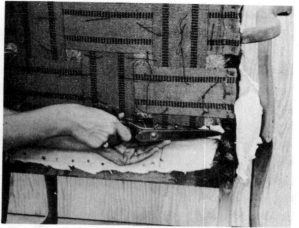

Fig. 13-2. Cutting Muslin to Fit Corner

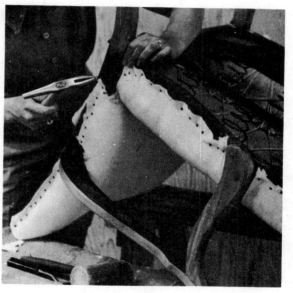

Fig. 13-3. Tacking Muslin Cover in Position

driven home. If this is done and the tack is slanted slightly, the edge of the tack may cut through the fabric. It is best to hit the tack until the head is almost to the fabric, and then to drive it home with one final blow.

Pleats and Folds

When pleats or folds are made they should always fold over toward the *outside* of the furniture or *downward*. These folds will not trap dust or dirt, making the cleaning job easier. Generally, several small folds of uniform size look neater than one large fold.

In pleating the front of a curved arm which is to be covered with a panel, make the pleats so that their edges will all point toward a central point. This improves their appearance. Here again, many small pleats will look better, and they are easier to make.

Folds or pleats on square or boxy furniture are the easiest type to make. The edge of the fold should align perfectly with the outer edge. In this situation the single fold may work quite well.

Corners

In making cuts in fabric for pulling it into corners or for fitting it around a projecting part such as the arm of an occasional chair, care must be taken not to cut too far into the fabric. The material should be cut part way, pulled into position, and checked to see how much further it needs to be cut. Note Fig. 13-2. Once the fabric is cut too far, the only remedy is to replace it with another new piece. This can be rather costly.

Removing Bumps

If the stuffing material was not applied very evenly, minor bumps can be removed while applying the muslin or even the final covering material. Sliding the hands over the surfaces and sighting from different angles will help locate bumps. They should be hit with the side of the upholsterer's hammer or the side of one's hand until eliminated. A stuffing regulator or a stiff needle can be used to remove stubborn bumps. Care should be exercised not to damage or soil the fabric.

Using Muslin

Covering overstuffed furniture with inexpensive unbleached muslin is considered good practice, Fig. 13-3. It not only makes a job of re-covering at a future date easier, but it also helps to give smooth contours and results in a longer life for the outer covering fabric by taking up some of the strain. Beginners, especially, will find that the addition of the muslin cover will make the job of upholstering easier and more enjoyable, particularly when they are applying the outside cover fabric.

chapter

14

Attaching Covers and Panels

When a person begins to examine the construction of a piece of upholstered furniture, he usually wonders how the covers and front panels are held in position without any tacks or nails being visible. The covers include the covering on the outside of the arms and on the rear side of the back. The process of attaching these in a manner which conceals the tacks is known in the trade as *blind tacking*.

Blind Tacking

To blind tack a cover, first hold the piece of fabric by the top corners and place it in the correct position. Be sure that it is centered so that there will be enough material at each end for tacking. Then flip the material up and over so it is reversed. Drive a tack in the center and then pull the fabric taut from one end and tack in place. Do the same with the other end. These three tacks will hold the top edge of the cover in place, as shown in Fig. 14-1.

Now cut a strip of cardboard ⅜ to ½ inch in width and as long as the width of the cover. Tack this over the three temporary tacks on the reverse side of the material. Keep the tacks

near the top edge of the cardboard to give a tight fit. See Figs. 14-2 and 14-3.

Next flip the cover back down so that the right side of the material is on the outside and in the correct position. Pull it down tightly at the center first, turn it under the bottom of the chair and tack it in position. Keep the tacks back from the edge so that they can be easily covered by the cambric later.

Fig. 14-1. Front Cover Panel Ready for Blind Tacking — Held by Three Tacks

95

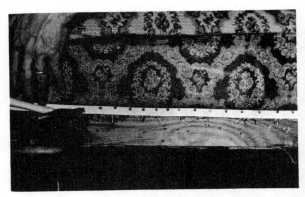

Fig. 14-2. Blind Tacking Through Cardboard Strip

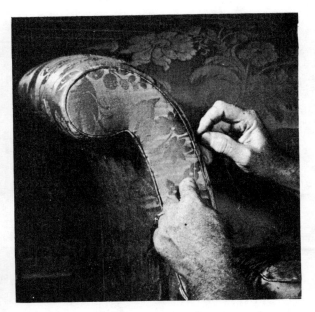

Fig. 14-4. Blind Stitching an Arm Panel (Kittinger)

Fig. 14-3. Blind Tacking a Side Cover with a Cardboard Strip

Finally, tack the sides of the cover with gimp tacks, starting near the top and working to the bottom. A superior job may be produced by blind stitching the sides using a curved needle.

Panels

Panels are used to cover the front arms and are usually made from plywood to prevent splitting and warping. They are padded with cotton felt and covered before being attached to the chair. Very short tacks (No. 1, 1½, or 2, depending upon the panel thickness) are used so they will not penetrate through the panel and scratch an unsuspecting lounger.

After the panels are covered, they are placed in position and small brads are driven right through the fabric on the panel to hold the panel to the frame of the chair. Care must be taken not to cut the fabric with the hammer head. The trick is to drive the brad carefully until the head is almost against the fabric and then to give it one sharp final blow. Be sure the face of the hammer is held parallel to the surface of the panel. A curved needle will aid in making the brad pop through the fabric if this isn't accomplished with the final hammer blow. Special brads can be obtained at an upholstery supply house. They have a conical head (similar to that of a casing nail) which allows them to slide through the fabric more readily than ordinary brads.

Occasionally front panels are made by tacking a stuffing material such as cotton directly to the frame and covering it with muslin and the covering fabric. The welting, the covering fabric for the inside of the arm, and the outside of the arm are then hand stitched in position using blind stitches. Note Fig. 14-4. This is a customary procedure in the manufacture of custom-made furniture and in the reproduction of antiques.

Sewing Welting and Cushions 15

Welting is the rolled edging used to finish off the edges of cushions, to hide seams, and to obtain decorative effects. Strips of fabric are cut to the desired width (1½ inches for a core 5/32 inch in diameter). To sew welting a special sewing machine attachment called a cording foot is used. The cording foot permits the sewing to be done very close to the cord, producing a firm, tight, rolled edge.

Sewing Welting

In sewing welting the following steps should be taken:

1. Seam the ends of two pieces together, face-to-face, about one-half inch from the ends. See Fig. 15-1. It is not necessary to use the cording foot.
2. Repeat Step 1 until all pieces are joined together to form one long continuous strip.
3. After placing the cording foot on the machine, wrap the fabric around the welting cord and begin sewing. Hold the unsewed portion at a slight angle to make the roll firm; however, don't have the angle too great or the cording foot will climb up on the welt.

Fig. 15-1. Sewing Two Pieces of Welting Together

Fig. 15-2. Sewing Welting at Seam

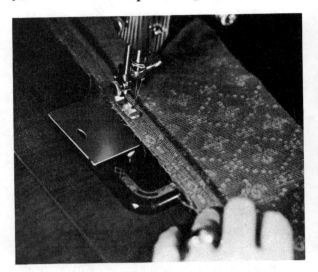

Fig. 15-3. Sewing Welting to Side of Cushion

Fig. 15-4. Sewing Top of Cushion to Side of Cushion

4. Open all seams as you come to them, as shown in Fig. 15-2. Sew slowly near the seam to prevent breaking a needle on the doubled thickness. Sew as close to the cord as possible to make the welt small.

Sewing Cushions

In sewing cushions the following steps should be taken:

1. Decide upon the cushion shape. It is better to design furniture so that rectangular cushions can be made. This type cushion not only can be reversed from top to bottom, but from front to back as well; this helps to maintain the original shape of the cushion by dividing the wear on the welted edges.

2. After the pieces are cut, sew the cushion side strips together—end-to-end to form a long narrow strip.

3. Sew welting to both top and bottom edges of this side strip, leaving three inches unsewed at each end, Fig. 15-3. Plan to have any seams in the welting come at the sides of the cushion and not in the front or rear.

4. Starting at the *side* of the top (or bottom) of the cushion, sew this part to the side strip with welting attached. See Fig. 15-4. Be sure the fabric is face to face. Again, do not sew the three inches at each end of the side strip.

5. Seam the ends of the side strips (the welting is unattached here) so that the sides fit properly as one continuous strip around the cushion.

6. Rip one end of the welting open; trim the other end off square and insert it inside the first. To eliminate any bulge, some of the welting cord can be trimmed away and the end of the fabric folded under and pulled tightly against the cording foot. Sew the welting so that it too is one continuous strip.

7. Join the welting to the side; then join it to the top (or bottom). An experienced cushion sewer may sew these together at the same time, but the beginner will find it easier to sew them separately.

8. Sew the last piece of the cushion, either bottom (or top), to the side. One end, plus a distance equal to the thickness of

the cushion on the two adjoining edges, is not sewed together, to allow room for the cushion to be stuffed. Turning in the edge of this piece and running a single seam about one-quarter inch from the folded edge makes it easier to sew the edge later after stuffing.

9. Stuff the cushion. This can be accomplished without an expensive cushion stuffing machine. Simply fold two pieces of heavy galvanized sheet iron into U shapes. Pieces 31″ to 33″ x 27″ before folding are a good size. The pieces are slipped over the cushion stuffing from opposite sides and pushed together. A piece of spring cord with a slip knot will aid in squeezing them together and holding them in position while the cushion cover is slipped into place. Remove the cord first, and then pull the galvanized pieces out separately while holding the stuffing in place. Standing the cushion on the floor and using your foot to hold the stuffing in place makes this easier to accomplish; however, be sure to put a clean piece of paper on the floor to protect the cushion.

10. Sew the open end of the cushion by hand, using sewing twine and a curved needle. Skewers will aid in holding the edges together for sewing. Seam stretchers, either the bar or chain type, are also helpful in this operation.

Foam Rubber and Its Fabrication 16

Foam rubber is used extensively in the construction of upholstered furniture. The ease with which it can be applied, its exceptional durability, the superior appearance provided by its tough uniform contour, and the comfort it gives in the finished piece of furniture offset its slightly higher cost.

It can be fabricated easily to form various sizes and shapes, and in the case of cushions it is available already molded in a variety of sizes and shapes. These include reversible, non-reversible (for built-in seat or back cushions), and T-shaped cushions. Foam rubber can be purchased in slab form, either solid or cored. It can be easily cut with hand shears or with a specially equipped band saw. Pieces can be joined quickly with rubber cement to form special shapes providing versatility in furniture design. Tacking tape can also be cemented to foam rubber to provide a means of tacking it to frames.

Characteristics

The following highly desirable features of foam rubber make it possible to use it to great advantage in upholstering furniture.

Resiliency

Foam rubber springs back immediately to its original shape as soon as any applied pressure is removed. This resilient characteristic means the furniture upholstered with foam rubber

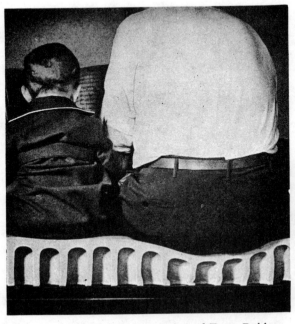

Fig. 16-1. Independent Suspension of Foam Rubber—Heavier Person Causes No Pull to Point of Greatest Deflection (U.S. Rubber)

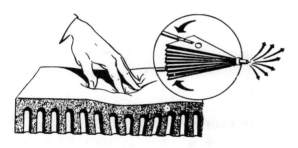

Fig. 16-2. Foam Rubber Aerates, or Breathes, by Bellows Action (U.S. Rubber)

maintains its neat appearance at all times. It eliminates the need for continual neatening and fluffing of cushions by the housewife. Its elasticity also provides firm, uniform, restful support as it gives with every movement of the body. Foam rubber also provides for independent suspensions with no pull to the point where the weight is greatest (the point of greatest deflection) nor drag toward the center which would give a hammock effect. Its independent suspension can be easily seen from Fig. 16-1. Foam rubber buoys up any weight, and pressure at every point of contact is equalized.

Durability

Foam rubber withstands rough treatment, and has withstood the test of time. Since 1931 it has been used in seat cushions on buses, trains, and airplanes during peacetime; and used in pads and cushions on tanks, trucks, airplanes, battleships, and special equipment in World War II and the Korean Conflict.

Rigid laboratory testing has shown that a foam rubber mattress after 10,000,000 compressions was in better shape than other types of mattresses after 250,000 compressions. Foam rubber does not sag or pack down. There is nothing in foam rubber to break down or lump up, and there are no springs to sag or break. Molded cushions hold their shape. However, foam rubber should be stored in a dark place

as long exposure to light will cause it to harden and crumble.

The smooth flowing contour of foam rubber increases the life of the fabric covering it. There are no sharp corners which usually wear first, and the resiliency of the foam rubber absorbs any shock from bumps or blows which might damage the fabric.

Economy

Foam rubber is economical when one considers that it results in a saving of both time and materials. Since it is a one-piece material it is easy to handle, making it unnecessary to spend time filling, picking out foreign matter, distributing and regulating separate materials. In using foam rubber fewer production steps are involved. It needs only to be placed in position and attached to the frame. No hand shaping is necessary as the shape is already molded. The fabric is also more easily and quickly fitted over accurately molded surfaces. Springs are eliminated in the case of cushions and in many other instances in seats and backs. With foam rubber there is no waste of stuffing material as every scrap can be used. Foam rubber also results in less need for replacement due to its great durability. If it is kept covered so that it is not exposed to the light, it will last indefinitely.

Sanitation

Foam rubber is hygienically clean and odorless. Because of its elasticity, it makes no dust itself, and its bellows action expels any dust, Fig. 16-2. This action also helps it to repel germs, moths, and vermin. Foam rubber is a mothproof material. In addition, it is an ideal material for persons with allergies.

Foam rubber is completely porous enabling it to "breathe" through its millions of tiny, interconnecting air cells, as seen in Fig. 16-3. Its cellular structure permits room temperature air to circulate freely throughout its entire form. This carries away body heat and (contrary to popular opinion) makes furniture cooler. Foam rubber actually absorbs body heat and "exhales" it.

Lightness

Foam rubber is amazingly light in weight since it is composed of 85 to 95 percent air. Therefore furniture in which it is used is easier to handle and move.

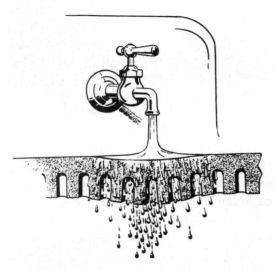

Fig. 16-3. Porosity of Foam Cushions Demonstrated (U.S. Rubber)

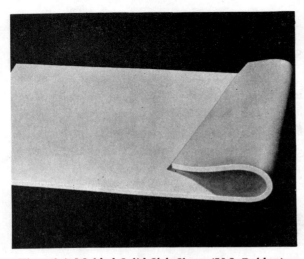

Fig. 16-4. Molded Solid Slab Sheet (U.S. Rubber)

Quietness

Being composed of only rubber and air, it does not creak or make other noises. In fact, it actually absorbs sound.

Moisture Resistance

Foam rubber is suitable for use in all climatic conditions since it is unaffected by changes in atmospheric temperature and humidity. This makes it resistant to mold and mildew. It remains dry even without use.

Versatility

The extreme versatility of foam rubber provides for design freedom. It can be bent, rolled, folded, cut, or cemented together to form any desired shape. In some cases it is even cemented directly to the frame surfaces. It can be used over any surface and in any style of furniture — wherever padding or upholstering is desired.

Forms

Foam rubber may be obtained in a wide variety of forms, shapes, sizes, and degrees of compression — from extremely soft to exceptionally firm. One manufacturer grades density as follows:

X Soft	(8-15 lbs.)	X Firm	(60-85 lbs.)
Soft	(15-25 lbs.)	XX Firm	(85-115 lbs.)
Medium	(25-40 lbs.)	XXX Firm	(115-150 lbs.)
Firm	(40-60 lbs.)	XXXX Firm	(150-200 lbs.)

It is available in sheet or slab form, either solid or cored; in molded forms for nonreversible cushions and seats; and in fully molded reversible cushion units.

Solid Slab

Solid slab sheets of foam rubber may be purchased for cutting to any desired shape, Fig. 16-4. It is available in thicknesses from 1/4 inch to 2 inches. Solid slabs measure 54 inches by 44 inches; however, 54-inch slabs are also available in the following thicknesses and lengths: 1 inch x 50 feet; ½ inch x 100 feet; ¼ inch x 200 feet.

Cored Slab

Molded, cored utility slab stock is made with molded openings in one side and is recommended for applications which call for depth and buoyancy, Fig. 16-5. In cored stock, a series of large, tube-like holes extend into the stock from its bottom surface. There are two principal reasons for the presence of the cores: first, the spacing and size of the cores help to control the density (degree of compressibility); and second, the cores provide a reduction in weight which is particularly important in aircraft applications and occasional furniture. Further, cores offer the added advantage of venting, and provide for greater resiliency. Cored slab is available in thicknesses ranging from ¾ inch to 4½ inches and in several densities. It may be used over any surface and in practically any application. Cored utility stock can be cut and cemented to form reversible cushions of any shape or size.

Cored Crowned

Crowned utility cored stock is cored stock with one side molded in a crowned shape, Fig. 16-6. Two identical halves may be cemented together to form a reversible cushion. The stock is available in 80-inch lengths by 2⅞ inches thick, and either 22¾- or 24¾-inch widths; it also can be purchased in 80-inch lengths by 2 9/16 inches thick and widths of the following measurements: 20, 21, 22, 23, 24, 26 and 28 inches.

Molded Cushion Units

Fully molded cushion units can be obtained ready to fit onto furniture without further cutting or shaping, Fig. 16-7. They may be

solid foam, half-cored, or cored through, depending on the purpose and the density required. Units can be obtained for tight seats, backs, arms, and reversible cushions, in a large variety of widths and lengths, sufficient to fit

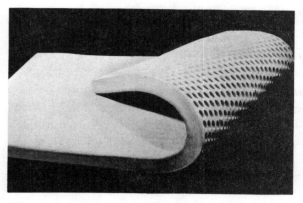

Fig. 16-5. Molded Cored Slab Sheet (U.S. Rubber)

Fig. 16-6. Crowned Utility Cored Stock (Goodyear)

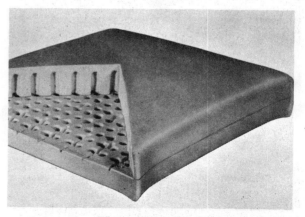

Fig. 16-7. Reversible Molded Cored Cushion (U.S. Rubber)

most chairs and sofas. Crown height is either 5⅛ or 5¾ inches, and boxing is either 3⅞ or 4 1/16 inches. Cushions are available in square, rectangular, T and L shapes. For specifications and prices on molded cushions and slab stock, contact your upholstery supplier or write directly to one of the latex foam manufacturers.

Fabrication of Foam Rubber

Foam rubber is easy to work with and requires little experience. Even beginners, with some degree of natural talent, can produce very satisfactory work. The use of foam rubber presents no problems of making additional space or purchasing elaborate equipment. As

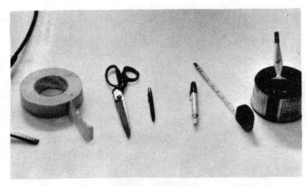

Fig. 16-8. Foam Rubber Fabricating Tools and Supplies (Schramm at Excelsior)

Fig. 16-9. Laying Out Using a Solid Pattern (Natural Rubber)

Fig. 16-8 shows, all that is needed to work with foam rubber is: a pair of heavy shears, a tape measure, a straightedge, a marking pen or pencil, foam rubber tape, cement, soapstone, and a flat work table. If power tools are available, such as a vertical or horizontal band saw, or a table cutting machine and portable buffer, fabricating work will quite naturally be speeded up.

Laying Out

The smooth "skin" of foam rubber provides a good surface on which to lay out pattern guide lines. Place the pattern on the foam rubber and draw around it with a China marking pencil as illustrated in Fig. 16-9. An indelible or colored pencil, or an inexpensive ball-point pen will work equally well. In using these, moisten the surface of the foam rubber slightly to make the lines darker and more legible. Some workmen prefer to dust talc through perforated patterns or around the edge of a solid pattern.

Latex Foam Manufacturers

Company	Product Name
American Foam Rubber Co., Burlington, New Jersey	"Mirafoam"
The Dayton Rubber Co., Dayton, Ohio	"Koolfoam"
Faultless Rubber Co., Ashland, Ohio	"Wonderfoam"
Firestone Tire & Rubber Co., Akron, Ohio	"Foamex"
Goodyear Tire & Rubber Co., Akron, Ohio	"Airfoam"
Hewitt-Robins, Inc., Buffalo, New York	"Restfoam"
Sponge Rubber Products Co., Shelton, Connecticut	"Texfoam"
United States Rubber Co., Rockefeller Center, New York, N. Y.	"U.S. Koylon Foam"

(Courtesy of Natural Rubber Bureau)

Cutting Allowances

As pointed out earlier, foam rubber is a highly resilient, buoyant material. Each cell, when subjected to any pressure, gives to accommodate that pressure, and springs back to its normal shape when the pressure is removed. Therefore, it is obvious that upholstery coverings should fit snugly and surface lines should be smooth and flowing. To achieve this highly desired feature, it is necessary to cut foam rubber slightly larger than the desired finished dimensions of the furniture piece or pattern. How much larger depends upon the type of piece you are upholstering. The following recommendations for widths of cutting allowances are suitable for most applications.

Note that these recommendations apply only to cushions made by hand. If fully molded reversible cushions are bought from a supplier, this allowance has already been provided. Take measurements accurately and specify finish size only.

Allow 1/4 inch on all sides for small pieces, such as dining room or wall chairs, and small or medium-sized one-cushion built-ins.

Allow 1/2 inch on all sides for regular, occasional or easy chairs, small love seats, three-cushion davenports or large built-ins.

Allow 3/4 inch on all sides for two-cushion davenports and extra large built-ins.

Allow 2 1/2 inches on length for davenports and built-ins with long one-piece cushions. Width allowance should be from 1/2″ to 3/4″. Wide cushions should have the larger allowance and narrower ones the smaller allowance.

This plan of oversizing can be modified according to the density of the foam rubber. If you are working with very soft (low compression) stock, increase the cutting allowance a little; if the stock is very firm, decrease it a slight amount.

Cutting with Hand Shears

Foam rubber may be cut easily with regular upholsterer's shears. See Fig. 16-10. The blades should be at least six inches long.

Solid slab foam rubber of any stock thickness can be cut clear through. The same applies to cored stock up to two inches in thickness. Some craftsmen prefer to make a through cut even with stock three inches thick. However, for material more than two inches in thickness the following procedure is recommended: first, make a cut from the smooth surface sufficiently deep to separate the top of each core, leaving only the core walls joined; second, as shown

Fig. 16-10. Cutting Thin Cored Stock with Shears (U.S. Rubber)

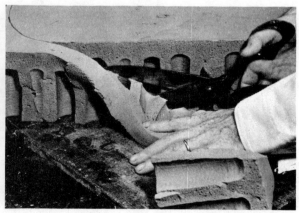

Fig. 16-11. Making Second Cut Through Thick Cored Stock (Goodyear)

in Fig. 16-11, cut through each core wall to complete the separation; third, trim off any rough spots. This method assures a true vertical cut.

When cutting heavy or high compression stock, lubricate your shears by dipping them in water frequently. If a beveled or slant edge is desired, it is best to make a vertical cut first, and then trim to the proper contour, Fig. 16-12. With a little practice a beginner will be able

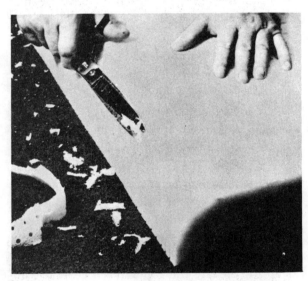

Fig. 16-12. Snipping a Rounded Edge (Schramm)

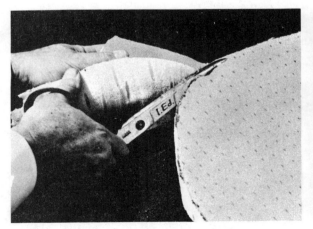

Fig. 16-13. A Rounded Corner (Schramm)

to get a perfectly rounded edge by snipping with the shears and buffing smooth with sandpaper or a buffing machine. See Fig. 16-13.

Cutting with Power Tools

Foam rubber lends itself well to cutting and contouring with table cutters and conventional band saws. These machines, of course, speed up the operations.

Table Cutters

Several types of table cutting machines are on the market. With this versatile instrument, straight cuts, curves and corners are easily cut. See Fig. 16-14. A clean edge is assured with any power cutter.

Vertical Band Saw

A *vertical band saw,* 14 inches or larger (the larger the better), with a conventional wood cutting blade, performs well in cutting foam rubber. Note Fig. 16-15. However, a special blade with a "bread knife" cutting edge will give a smoother cut with less tendency to pucker the stock. If a blade wider than 1/4 inch is used, a guide or guard should be installed to move the cut stock away from the blade; this reduces

Fig. 16-14. Cutting a Curve with a Table Cutter
(Schramm at Excelsior)

Fig. 16-15. Cutting Solid Slab Stock on a Bandsaw (Schramm at Excelsior)

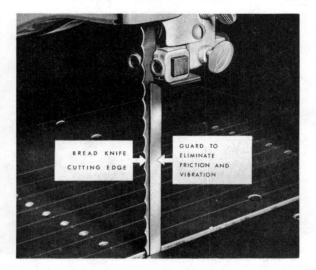

Fig. 16-16. Bandsaw with Bread-Knife Blade and Special Guard (U.S. Rubber)

frictional drag and the tendency to pinch the blade, Fig. 16-16.

The larger the saw, the more latitude provided in handling wider material. To cut material that is wider than the saw clearance use an extension table bolted or clamped to the saw table. This allows you to support the stock and to do your cutting on the outside or the right side of the blade with the scrap inside. If an extension table is not used, the excess material can be rolled up.

To enable the foam rubber to slide, wax the saw table or sprinkle soapstone on it. A piece of waxed or wrapping paper placed under the foam rubber will also prove advantageous.

With a tilt-table arrangement on your saw, you can easily make desired angle and template cuts. See Fig. 16-17.

Horizontal Band Saw

The *horizontal band saw* is frequently used by large producers. Specializing in mass production of high-style custom furniture, large maufacturers usually order a sufficient quantity of an item to justify a custom mold. However, when special shapes and surface curvatures are

Fig. 16-17. Making a Beveled Cut on a Bandsaw (Schramm at Excelsior)

needed in a variation of sizes on a "special" basis, upholsterers who cater to this type of business have found that the horizontal band saw is a valuable tool, Fig. 16-18. Foam rubber distributors often have equipment to fabricate special jobs. Contact them through your supplier, and work out your specifications with them, or you may want to fabricate your own special shapes; this will be explained later in the text.

Fig. 16-18. Cutting Solid Stock on a Horizontal Bandsaw (Schramm at Excelsior)

Fig. 16-19. Rounding Corners on a Buffer (Goodyear)

Buffing Wheel

A power buffer, 3 to 4 inches wide, can be used to advantage for smoothing edges or rounding a radius. See Fig. 16-19. Proceed very cautiously when applying pressure, until you are familiar with the operation. As mentioned earlier, this operation can also be performed by hand using sandpaper.

Cementing Foam Rubber

The ease with which foam rubber can be cemented to itself, to tacking tape, or to wood, metal, plastics, or fabrics provides an outstanding advantage to fabricators. It enables them to develop a wide variety of shapes and sizes, to adapt foam rubber to innumerable applications, and to utilize all scrap pieces of the material.

Cement for Foam Rubber

Fabricating cement (used for joining foam rubber to foam rubber or to tacking tape) comes in two separate containers; one is the cement proper, the other is an activator which speeds up the setting action of the cement. Note Fig. 16-20. The two parts do not come already mixed because the mixture will gel within twenty-four hours. Therefore, only a

sufficient quantity to handle the needs of one day should be mixed at one time. If necessary, the life of the activated cement mixture can be prolonged several days by placing it in a refrigerator to retard the setting action. The mixture will provide a good bond until it becomes too thick to spread. However, once it has gelled, it cannot be reclaimed by adding a solvent or a fresh mixture to it.

The activator should be added in the proportion of ten cubic centimeters (about one-third of an ounce) to each pint of cement. The

Fig. 16-20. Cement and Activator (Natural Rubber)

activator has some thinning action, but if more fluid consistency is desired, lead-free gasoline may be added. For best results, add the thinner to the unmixed cement; then add the activator.

Cementing Rubber to Rubber

To cement foam rubber to foam rubber, first coat the surface of each piece lightly with activated cement. Allow the surfaces to become tacky; this normally requires from three to five minutes. Bring the pieces together lightly at first so that adjustments can be made in position. When the pieces are exactly in position, press them together firmly for a few seconds. Within several minutes the joint will be sufficiently bonded to allow working with the material. However, severe handling should not be attempted for several hours. Before being put into use, all seams should be allowed to dry at least overnight.

Cementing Rubber to Tape

To cement foam rubber to tacking tape spread a thin coat of activated cement to the foam rubber one inch from the edge. Allow a minute or two for drying, then register the tape in place as shown in Fig. 16-21. Tacking tape aids accurate edging; it secures the foam rubber to the base, and at the same time reinforces the edges, Fig. 16-22. It comes in varying widths with a one-inch coating of special adhesive. For reinforcing two joined sections of foam rubber, a special full-coated tape is obtainable, or regular tape may be used by applying cement to the uncoated portion.

Cementing Rubber to Other Materials

Cement used for bonding foam rubber permanently to a wood, metal, or plastic base comes ready to use in one container. It is applied the same as ordinary wood glue is, by coating both surfaces, allowing them to

Fig. 16-21. Attaching Tape to Foam Rubber (Schramm at Excelsior)

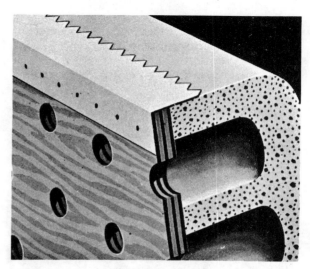

Fig. 16-22. Foam Rubber Taped and Tacked to Plywood Base (Dunlop)

become tacky, and then setting them into place with a little pressure applied. Permanent drying requires several hours.

Dusting Powder

Inexpensive commercial soapstone, or ordinary talcum powder, is useful in fabricating foam rubber. Dust it on table tops when handling large sections of foam rubber to permit easy sliding. Rub it on cushion units to eliminate friction in automatic filling machines, and to facilitate slip cover adjustment. Sprinkle it lightly over any excess areas that have been

Fig. 16-23. Dusting Cored Stock with Soapstone
(Schramm)

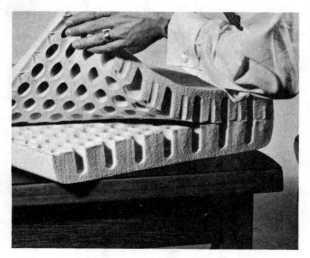

Fig. 16-24. Cementing the Two Halves Together
(Goodyear)

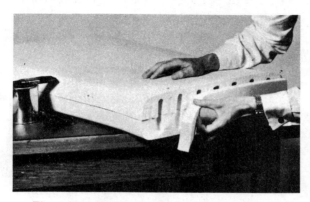

Fig. 16-25. Positioning End Slab (Goodyear)

accidentally cemented, especially when they are likely to come in contact with covering materials or other foam rubber. Soapstone absorbs any excess cement which may have been applied. When exposed core edges are to be cemented together, dust soapstone in the cores to absorb excess cement and to prevent the core cells from sticking together or collapsing. See Fig. 16-23.

Fabricating Reversible Cushions

Reversible or loose cushions may be made from cored stock by any of four different methods:

Method One

Use crown utility stock, plus a small amount of soft, solid slab stock.

1. Purchase crown stock half as thick as the crown dimension desired at the center of the cushion. It should be as wide as the cushion. Be sure to add the usual upholstery allowances to assure a snug fit. (See "Cutting Allowances" in this chapter.)

2. Cut two pieces of the stock, each 2 inches shorter than the length of the finished cushion, taking into consideration the upholstery allowance.

3. Bevel the bottom edge at each end with shears. This reduces thickness and produces a crowned effect at the ends of the finished cushion. In some applications, the beveling operation is not needed if the resulting difference in crowns at the ends is acceptable.

4. Cement the two halves together making sure they are evenly aligned and not distorted, Fig. 16-24. (See "Cementing Foam Rubber" in this chapter.)

5. Cut two pieces of one-inch, soft, solid slab, two inches less in width than the crown height desired at the ends of the

cushion, and two inches shorter than the width of the cushion.

6. Cement these strips to the ends of the cushion, centering them in relation to the top and bottom surfaces and from side to side, Fig. 16-25. The cores should be dusted with soapstone and the cement applied to both surfaces, before the strips are cemented.

7. Apply cement to the edges of the slab strips and of the crown stock. (The edges of the strips should form right angles with the boxing edges.)

8. Gently press the edges together to get the effect of a full rounded contour for both top and bottom surfaces and the corners. Let the cement dry thoroughly for an hour or two before severe handling, and overnight before covering. A cross section of the operation is pictured in Fig. 16-26.

Method Two

Use flat cored utility stock, plus a small amount of solid slab stock (Fig. 16-27).

1. Purchase flat cored stock thick enough that when doubled it will give the required height at the crown of the cushion. Always

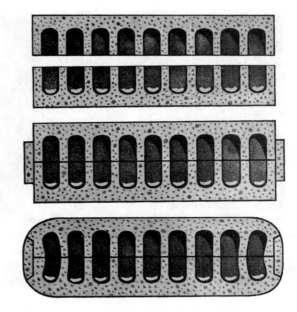

Fig. 16-26. Cross Section of Fabricated Reversible Cushion Showing Steps of Construction (Dunlop)

calculate upholstery allowances.

2. Cut two pieces of stock, 2 inches less in width and length than the finished size of the cushion, remembering upholstery allowances.

3. Cut four strips of 1-inch soft slab stock to a width of 2 inches less than the crown height of the cushion and to a length equal to that of the cushion side.

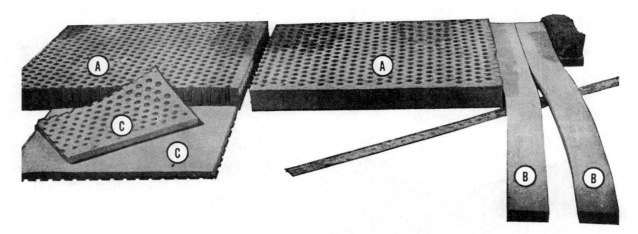

Fig. 16-27. Foam Rubber Stock for Fabricating a Reversible Cushion (Goodyear)
A. Flat cored utility stock   B. Soft solid slab stock   C. Cored utility stock (soft slab stock may be used)

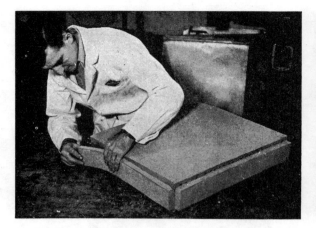

Fig. 16-28. Applying Slabs to Sides (Goodyear)

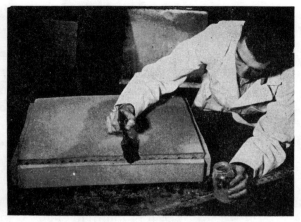

Fig. 16-29. Cementing Exposed Edges (Goodyear)

4. Cement and join the two pieces of cored stock together.

5. Cement the strips of plain slab stock and place them around the four sides of the cored stock, spacing equally from top and bottom. See Fig. 16-28.

6. Cement exposed edges of cored and slab stock and, when tacky, pinch together, Fig. 16-29.

Method Three

Use two pieces of cored utility stock.

1. Purchase two pieces of stock that are larger in width and length than the finished size of the cushion. When cemented together, they should give the required thickness at the crown. The over-allowance will vary with the thickness of the stock and depth of the bevel.

2. Bevel all four edges on the cored side of each piece as pictured in Fig. 16-30.

3. Cement the pieces together, smooth side out.

Method Four

Use two pieces of cored utility stock, plus a smaller amount of one-inch cored or solid slab stock. This method gives a firmer cushion with a high crown.

1. Purchase two pieces of cored utility stock which when doubled will give a thickness 1 inch less than the crown thickness. The pieces should be 2 inches less in width and length than the finished size of the cushion.

2. In a sandwich style, cement a piece of 1-inch cored utility stock or solid slab

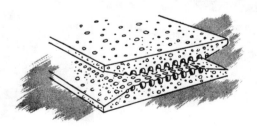

Fig. 16-30. Cross Section Showing Cored Utility Stock Beveled on All Four Edges (Natural Rubber)

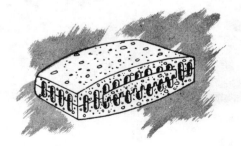

Fig. 16-31. Cross Section Showing Insertion of Extra Slab for Higher Crown and Firmer Cushion (Natural Rubber)

stock between the two pieces of cored stock. The piece should be about 2 inches less in width and length than that of the cored stock.

3. Cement 1-inch thick solid slab stock on all four sides, centering them carefully.

4. Join all edges together. Fig. 16-31 is a cross-section of the finished cushion.

Altering Molded Reversible Cushions

The sizes and shapes of regular molded reversible cushions may be altered easily. The method recommended is called the *end splice;* it is used to reduce or increase one or even two dimensions of a cushion. As the term "end splice" implies, the cushion to be altered is cut near one side to change the side-to-side measurement. If the front-to-back measurement is to be changed, the cut should be made near the rear boxing. A cut should not be made near the front edge or through the middle section, because these areas receive the most pressure while in use.

It is preferable to make the splice about 3 inches in from the cushion edge. Most of the taper occurs from that point to the edge; therefore, a splice in the area beyond is least disturbing to the contour of the cushion.

Applications of this method are as varied as the dimensions of cushions in the furniture industry today. A few typical examples of a general nature are offered here.

Reducing a Dimension

To reduce the size of a cushion, make a cut through the entire cushion about 3 inches in from the edge. The use of a vertical band saw or table cutter would make this operation easier but it can be readily done with hand shears.

Cut away the excess from the large piece in the same manner. See Fig. 16-32. Cement the end section (piece cut off first) and the main section together, being sure to align them carefully, Fig. 16-33. Use soapstone in the open cored sections.

Increasing a Dimension

To increase a dimension, slab stock can be used to increase a cushion up to 2 inches. Various thicknesses of slab stock can be cemented together to make up the desired thickness of the insert. For increases beyond 2 inches, it is recommended that a larger size stock cushion be used or that the cushion be fabricated from cored utility stock as explained earlier.

The procedure for increasing a dimension follows:

1. Purchase slab stock for the insert of the same compression as that of the cushion.
2. Cut the end section from the cushion 3 inches from the edge.
3. Cut the slab stocks.

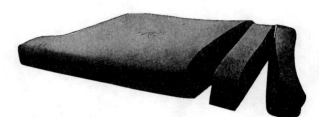

Fig. 16-32. Cuts Made for Removal of Center Section (Goodyear)

Fig. 16-33. Joining End Section to Main Section (Goodyear)

If desired, a pattern may be made on the insert by placing the fresh-cut edge of the cushion upon the slab stock and marking. See Fig. 16-34.

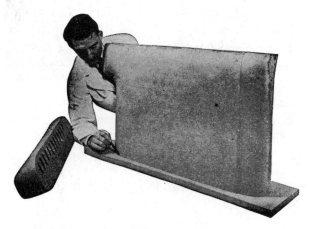

Fig. 16-34. Tracing Pattern on Insert (Goodyear)

Fig. 16-35. Insert Cemented to Main Section (Goodyear)

Fig. 16-36. Trimming Insert (Goodyear)

If no pattern is used, cut the slab stock in a rectangle to meet the dimensions needed. It may be easier to cut slightly oversize and trim to fit.

4. Cement the slab insert and the large section of the cushion together, being sure the slab extends flush to all edges (Fig. 16-35). Use soapstone in the cores, apply cement, and make contact with the cushion in a natural position. Don't compress it. Let it dry for a few minutes.

5. If a pattern was not made on the insert, trim the insert to conform with the contour of the cushion. See Fig. 16-36. Lightly buff the cemented edges.

6. Cement the end section to the unit. With the sections placed on a smooth surface, align the end section carefully with the original cut at every point. Apply gentle pressure from each end and allow to dry for a few minutes. Note Fig. 16-37.

Increasing a Dimension at the Boxing

Add soft slab stock to the original stock reversible cushion. Cut a piece of slab stock, thick enough to give the required new dimension, as wide as the crown dimension at the edge of the cushion and as long as the side

Fig. 16-37. Cementing End to Insert (Goodyear)

Fig. 16-38. Slab Adhered to Edge of Cushion
(Goodyear)

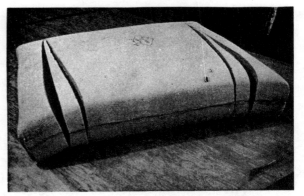

Fig. 16-39. Pie Cuts for Taper (Goodyear)

of the cushion to which it will be cemented. The edges should be flush. A centerline drawn on the slab piece will aid in positioning it. Apply cement to the slab and the edge of the boxing. Register them so that the mold line of the cushion meets the centerline of the slab. Then apply cement in the angles formed by the slab edge and the cushion. Press the edges of the slab against the surface of the cushion. When these adhere the effect of a full rounded contour is obtained as Fig. 16-38 illustrates. When increasing a dimension more than 1 inch, place equal thicknesses of slab on each side for best results.

Tapering a Rectangular Cushion

Remove two wedge-shaped pieces and rejoin the remaining sections. This method is similar to the method explained earlier to reduce the size of a cushion except that the excess material cut out will be a pie-cut to produce the required taper. Make the first cut parallel with the edge, starting at the back and ending about two inches from the front edge. Divide the total reduction by two, so that half of the reduction will be provided by each pie-cut. Mark the distance in from the first cut at the back edge. Make the second cut from this point to the point where the first cut ends. See Fig. 16-39. Guide lines may be drawn with a ball-point pen to provide greater accuracy in cutting.

Fig. 16-40. Finished Tapered Unit (Goodyear)

Cement the two sections together being careful to align the edges. Follow the same procedure for the other side. Note Fig. 16-40. For a one-inch taper, a stock cushion unit large enough for the front of the cushion can be pulled in by the cover without any altering of the cushion unit.

Fabricating Tight Cushioning

Tight cushioning includes all types of seats and backs that are in a fixed position under the covering. It includes the upholstering of occasional chairs, wall chairs, dining room chairs, built-ins, bunk seats, church pews, automotive and transportation seating, tight-cushion period chairs, settees and davenports, and a host of other applications, Fig. 16-41.

The ideal cushions for tight seats are half-sections of stock reversible cushions. Suppliers can furnish them, since stock reversible cushions are molded in half-sections that are later bonded together to produce full molded cushions. These half-sections have a built-in crown, and they taper uniformly to all edges. Sizes can be

Fig. 16-41. Tight Cushioned Chair with Seats and Back in Fixed Position under Covering (Schramm at Lansburgh)

Fig. 16-42. Facing a Beveled Edge (Schramm)

altered by the same methods described previously for altering standard reversible cushions.

Tight cushioning for all types of seating can be made with foam rubber utility stock in essentially the same manner. The basic steps include: (1) make a pattern; (2) cut foam rubber from the pattern; (3) register the foam rubber in position on the frame and attach it permanently, if necessary; and (4) apply the covering.

To fabricate a tight cushion unit from cored utility stock, it is preferable to cover all exposed core surfaces (except the bottom) with a layer of smooth solid slab stock. This affords reinforcement at the edges where extra strength is usually needed. Beveled or slant edges should be faced to withstand the additional strain. See Fig. 16-42. Facing also makes the edges uniform and assures top-quality appearance for the finished job.

Generally, 1-inch soft slab stock is used for the facing plate, although lesser thicknesses can be used, according to the service the piece is expected to perform. If facing is to be done, the thickness of the slab stock must be considered in the overall dimensions of the unit and the dimensions of the main section decreased accordingly.

To face the exposed cores of a cushion, simply cut a piece of slab stock to fit, or use scrap cuttings, and cement the surfaces together. The rough edges are trimmed after cementing, and the desired radii needed at the corners can be obtained by sanding or buffing.

A facing is not required when the cored stock is to be taped at the edges and tacked in place as in an arm rest or when a cushioned or contoured edge is to be used. These will be described in the next chapter.

Upholstering with Foam Rubber

The ease with which foam rubber can be utilized in upholstering processes and its great versatility in varied applications make it an ideal material. The preliminary upholstering steps, such as frame preparation and the construction of foundations or supporting platforms, are essentially the same as those followed in conventional upholstery practices. The greatest difference found in the use of foam rubber is the elimination of the most difficult part of conventional methods — the preparation, application, and regulation of the stuffing materials. This chapter covers the general applications of foam rubber and provides specific illustrations for a wide range of upholstering problems.

Mounting Foam Rubber

Foam rubber may be mounted over many different kinds of foundations, such as plywood, sheet metal, springs, and webbing. When mounting foam rubber over hard surfaces, provision must first be made for the foam rubber to breathe. This can be done by perforating the bases with one-quarter inch holes. Metal bases should be covered with a rust-resistant finish. Cut and position the foam rubber on the foundation and secure it by cementing it to the base or by tacking through tacking tape applied around the edges, as shown in Fig. 17-1.

When mounting foam rubber over springs, the springs should first be encased with a protective covering of burlap. An additional layer of cotton felt or sisal will insulate the foam rubber from the rubbing action of the springs and will prevent it from sagging down through the springs, resulting in longer life and greater comfort. The foam rubber should then be positioned over the cotton, felt, or sisal. See Fig. 17-2.

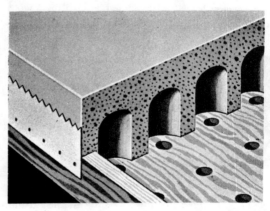

Fig. 17-1. Foam Rubber on Hard Surface (Dunlop)

117

The application of foam rubber cushioning over webbing is extremely simple. Space the webbing sufficiently far apart ($\frac{1}{4}''$) to allow adequate ventilation, and secure the cushion with tacking tape to the edges of the frame, Fig. 17-3.

Flexible platforms suspended by helical springs may also be used as bases for reversible cushions. See Fig. 17-4. The base is formed by a series of small helical tension springs around the sides of the frame. These support a layer of #10 duck fabric, as shown in Fig. 17-5. One loop at the end of each spring is hooked through a metal tab which is tacked to the frame. The loop at the other end of the spring passes through the fabric and around a wire border that has been double stitched into the fabric.

The springs are $1\frac{1}{4}$-inch coil springs, 14-gauge wire, $\frac{5}{8}$ inch O.D. The wire border is $\frac{1}{8}$-inch diameter or 10 gauge. Metal straps or wires may be used in place of the duck fabric. See Figs. 17-6 and 17-7.

Forming Edges

The inherent flexibility of foam rubber permits one to make any type of edge finish with a

Fig. 17-2. Foam Rubber on Springs (Dunlop)

Fig. 17-3. Foam Rubber on Webbing (Dunlop)

Fig. 17-4. Molded Foam Rubber Reversible Cushion over Flexible Platform (Goodyear)

Fig. 17-5. Flexible Platform Supported by Helical Springs (Goodyear)

minimum of work. Types of edges which may be formed include the square edge, the cushioned edge, and the feathered edge. When using cored stock, it is unnecessary to face it with solid slab stock as reinforcement is provided through the tacking tape, and only the smooth skin surface is exposed when pulled down in position.

Square Edges

Attach tacking tape flat against the stock edge and tack the tape overhang to the base. It is preferable to tack to the underneath side of the base wherever possible so that tack heads will not interfere with a smooth contour. For a square edge mounted over a box base, cut the stock to the dimensions of the outer edge of the box base, adding the 1/4-inch upholstery allowance all around, Fig. 17-8. Then mark the stock for the thickness of the box material and the depth of the box, so that it will fit over the edge of the box. Cut the foam rubber as marked. Cement the tacking tape in place and tack the overhang to the side of the box.

Fig. 17-6. Metal Straps Supported by Helical Springs (Goodyear)

Cushioned Edges

Cut the stock to the shape and size of the cushion, adding the customary 1/4 inch all around for upholstering allowance *plus 1/2 inch for edging allowance* (total of 3/4 inch over

Fig. 17-7. Interlaced Metal Wires Supported by Helical Springs (Goodyear)

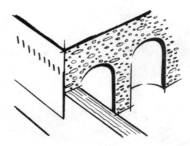

Fig. 17-8. Square Edge with Box Base (Goodyear)

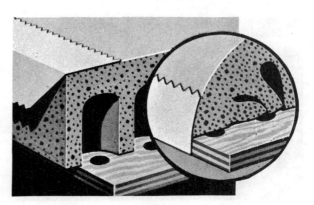

Fig. 17-9. Cushioned Edge (Dunlop)

base measurement at cushion edge). Cement the tape to the top surface of the foam rubber, 1 inch in from the edge. Tuck the bottom edge of the cushion under so that the edge is flat against the base. Smooth it in place as you go along and take care to keep the tape taut so that the foam rubber doesn't wrinkle or bunch unevenly. Make sure the edge hugs the edge of the base. Finally tack tape to base. See Fig. 17-9.

Feathered Edges

This type edge differs from the cushioned edge in that the curvature is more gradual. Cut the stock to the proper cushion size including the 1/4-inch upholstery allowance all around. Bevel the lower edge to the necessary degree to obtain the desired contour. For long

tapers increase the bevel. Cement the tacking tape to the top surface of the foam rubber, 1 inch from the edges. Draw the tape down so that the beveled edge of the cushion is flat against the base; tack in place. See Fig. 17-10.

Fabricating a High Crowned Cushion

Slab cored utility stock can be used to obtain a higher crown than that made by a cushioned or feathered edge. Select stock as thick as you wish the crown to be at the center of the cushion. Place the stock on a smooth flat surface with the bottom surface up. Mark the desired cushion thickness onto the side of the stock. (Measure up from the table and make the usual upholstery allowance.) Draw a line from this mark to the point where the taper is to begin. Repeat for the other side. See Fig. 17-11.

Begin cutting at the edge following the pattern lines drawn on the sides. Trim a little at a time, rather than making large cuts that might go too deep, Fig. 17-12. Do the same with the other side. If you have a buffer, you can smooth rough edges easily. However, the desired effect can be obtained satisfactorily with a hand shears. Register the cushion in position. Spot cement the bottom area where the tapers occur

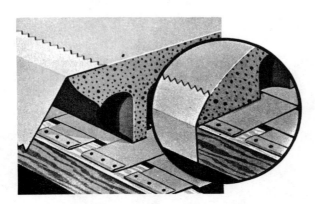

Fig. 17-10. Feathered Edge (Dunlop)

Fig. 17-11. Marking the Tapers (Schramm)

Fig. 17-12. Removing Excess Material (Schramm)

to keep a permanent crowned shape. Make the desired type of edge, and the cushion is ready to cover, Fig. 17-13.

Another method may be used to fabricate a high-crowned contour, fixed cushion. See Fig. 17-14. Select cored utility stock as thick as you wish the measurement at the boxing. Cut layers of solid slab stock in graduated sizes. Use as many layers as needed to give the required crown height at the center of the cushion. The edges of the smallest piece should come at the point where the taper is to begin on the cushion. The edges of the outer pieces should terminate at equal distances between the edge of the small piece and the edge of the cushion to give a uniform gradual contour. Cement the largest layer in the center of the bottom of the cushion. Then center and cement the other layers similarly as illustrated in Fig. 17-15. Trim the lower edges of each layer, if necessary, to help the contour. Spot cement the cushion in position and it is ready for covering. Note Fig. 17-16.

If the cushion is to be crowned in all directions, the tapers need to be built in at the front and back edges as well as the two sides. For best results with tight or fixed cushions, it is recommended that the front edge, where thickness is needed and flexing is frequent, be kept as high as possible.

In some instances, contouring from the top surface may be practical. When this is done a layer of solid slab stock is cemented to the top of the trimmed cored stock. Select cored stock the thickness of the crown dimension at

Fig. 17-14. Cored Stock Raised with Slab Stock
(Schramm)

Fig. 17-15. Cementing Slab Layers in Position
(Schramm)

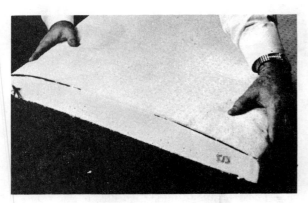

Fig. 17-13. Cushion Ready for Covering (Schramm)

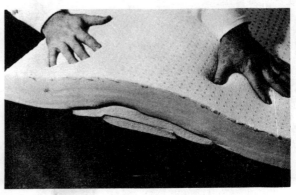

Fig. 17-16. Cushion Ready for Covering (Schramm)

Fig. 17-17. Trimming Cored Stock to
Desired Contour (Schramm)

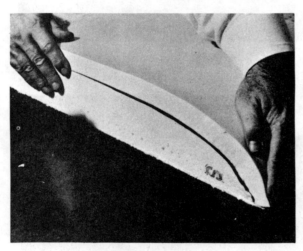

Fig. 17-18. Cementing Top Slab to Cored Stock
(Schramm)

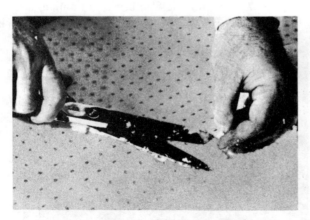

Fig. 17-19. Trimming Excess from Bottom of
Saddle Cushion (Schramm)

center of cushion less the thickness of the solid slab to be used on top. Fig. 17-17 shows how to trim the top of the cored stock to the desired contour. Cement the solid slab stock to the top surface of the cored stock, Fig. 17-18. Tape and tack in position ready for covering.

Producing a Saddle Effect

It is possible to obtain a saddle effect (inverted crown) with foam rubber mounted on a flat surface platform. Merely trim out the desired contour from the center of the *bottom surface* of the material. See Fig. 17-19. Cement the cushion firmly to the platform as Fig. 17-20 shows.

To cover concave cushions, cement the covering material to the foam rubber to make it cling to the contour and maintain a neat appearance.

Foam Rubber for Seats

Many types of seats may be upholstered with foam rubber using either solid slab or cored utility stock. Soft, medium, or firm densities may be used depending upon the particular application. They may be mounted over either solid, semi-flexible, or flexible platforms depending upon the required use and comfort desired.

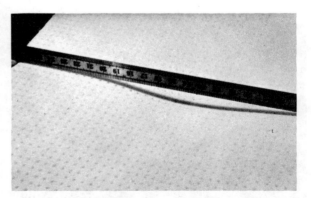

Fig. 17-20. Saddle Cushion Cemented to Platform
(Schramm)

Slip Seats

Hard slip seats can be made with plywood, metal, hard plastic, or heavy fiberboard bases such as those used in dining room or card table chairs, benches, and built-ins. With this seat type use solid slab stock of medium or firm compression either ¾-inch or 1-inch thick. Be sure to provide for free air passage by drilling ¼-inch or ⅜-inch holes at frequent intervals. Expanded metal bases also provide good platforms for foam rubber applications as shown in Fig. 17-21.

Fig. 17-21. Expanded Metal Seat (Goodyear)

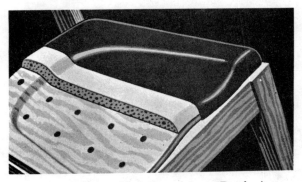

Fig. 17-22. Padded Shaped Seat (Dunlop)

Contour Seats

For pan, bucket, and saddle seats, or the new contour furniture which is molded to fit body curvatures, use cored utility stock at least 2 inches thick with a #2 compression. The foam rubber should be well cemented to the base and to the covering so that the fabric will follow the contours and not wrinkle or creep. See Fig. 17-22.

Recessed Platforms

With recessed rigid platforms, there is an opportunity to build in a luxurious cushioning effect. Make a notch cut around the perimeter of the foam rubber so that it fits into the well and extends flush with the frame on all sides. Note Fig. 17-23. Use #3 compression stock. The thickness of the foam rubber should be at least twice that of the depth of the recess; slightly more is better.

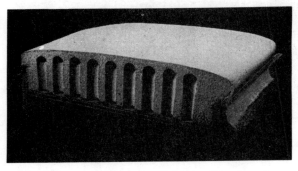

Fig. 17-23. Recessed Solid Base (Goodyear)

Built-In Benches

In cushioning built-in benches, 1-inch slab stock of soft or medium density can be used over a solid base which has small holes drilled at frequent intervals. Cored utility stock, medium or firm density (compression #3 through #4½), and at least 2 inches in thickness can also be used for benches, Fig. 17-24.

Fig. 17-24. Built-In Bench with Cored Stock (Dunlop)

Thin Seats

For thin seats, such as occasional or wall chairs and some built-ins, cored utility or solid slab stock can be used. When using cored stock a compression of #3 or #3½ is desirable; for solid stock a medium or firm density is best. The attractive wall chair in Fig. 17-25

Fig. 17-25. Wall Chair (Schramm at Lansburgh)

Fig. 17-26. Non-Reversible Seat and Back Using Cored Foam Rubber (Goodyear)

has a burlap and web-reinforced construction. Cored utility stock 2½ inches thick was spot-cemented in place and finished with a cushioned edge.

Deep Cushions

For deep seat cushions over all types of bases use cored utility stock, #3 through #4 compression depending on the flexibility desired, and at least 1 inch in thickness. A 3-inch thickness is commonly used, while a 4½-inch thickness will provide lounging comfort.

Foam Rubber for Backs

Both solid slab and cored utility stock are used for upholstering the backs of furniture pieces. The solid slab stock is usually used on smaller chairs and sometimes on built-in benches. Solid stock of soft density (compression load tolerance of 15 to 25 lbs.) is commonly used in thicknesses of ½ inch, ¾ inch, and 1 inch for dining room chair backs. On the backs of built-in benches, the thickness may be increased for greater comfort. Use tacking tape for anchoring at edges and cement the slab lightly to the back platform to keep it in position permanently. If the back platform is solid, be sure to provide air holes.

Cored utility stock is frequently used for backs on upholstered chairs, sofas, and many built-ins. The thicknesses vary from 1 inch to over 3½ inches depending upon the type of platform construction and the comfort desired. Thinner thicknesses are used over coil springs, while the thicker stock is employed directly over webbing, or over canvas, duck, or heavy burlap supported by metal straps. When spring construction is used, an insulation of cotton or sisal should be placed between the foam rubber and the burlap spring covering, Fig. 17-26.

For reversible backs and seats, thin stock, either cored or solid, is used in combination

Fig. 17-27. Reversible Back and Seat Using Cored Stock and Molded Cushion Units (Goodyear)

Fig. 17-28. Chair Arm Covered with Cored Foam Rubber (Natural Rubber)

with molded foam rubber cushion units. The procedure is the same as for non-reversible backs described above, except thinner stock is used. The cushion unit is then placed against this platform. Note Fig. 17-27.

Foam Rubber for Arms

The arms of chairs and sofas may be upholstered with either solid slab foam rubber or cored utility slab stock, depending upon the size of the arm and the amount of flexibility desired, Fig. 17-28. When using solid slab stock, a thickness of ¾ inch to 1 inch of soft or medium density is usually used; this is applied directly or over cotton felt. Cored foam rubber utility stock is usually used where greater resiliency is desired and on larger arms.

Piping, Buttoning, and Tufting

The journeyman upholsterer is, of course, familiar with the art of piping, buttoning, and tufting to create tailored pieces of unusual beauty. His ability in these and other special procedures determines his position as a master craftsman. An example of the use of piping is shown in Fig. 17-29. In the past, the intricate designs, varied contours, and the subsequent work of inserting the upholstering material, all contributed to the time consuming nature of

Fig. 17-29. Channel Back Occasional Chair (Mastland)

this task and made it a prohibitive undertaking, except in high-priced custom furniture. The introduction of foam rubber has changed all this.

An amateur with a little patience is able to produce professional looking work through the use of this one-piece material of uniform thickness. The pattern must still be made and the covering material cut, sewed and fitted to the base. However, the use of foam rubber eliminates the tedious jobs of tying and binding shredded bits of stuffing material together, prodding them into place, pulling out a section here and there to accommodate the contours, and holding the operation in place as it progressed (a procedure that always welcomed extra hands).

Piping Fabrication

Use cored utility stock for best results. The large cores offer the needed softness, yet resiliently hug the confining fabric to produce a permanently plump effect.

Dimensions and Compression of Cored Utility Stock for Pipes

Finished Pipe Size	Airfoam Thickness	Airfoam Compression	
		Over Springs	Over Webbing
Up to 4"	1½"	No. 1	No. 2
4" – 5½"	2"	No. 1	No. 1 or 2
5½" – 8"	2½"	No. 1	No. 1
8" and over	3"	No. 1	No. 1

(Courtesy Goodyear Tire and Rubber Co.)

Dimensions of Pipes

For the pipe width, a good general rule to follow is to cut the foam rubber the same width as the front of the covering fabric. For example, a pipe measuring 4½ inches across the back, with 6 inches of covering material needed to follow the curvature of the pipe, would require a piece of foam rubber stock 6 inches wide.

The length of the foam rubber from top to bottom depends, of course, upon the type of finished top edge that is planned. If it rolls generously over the top edge and feathers down the back, the additional length to accomplish this must be considered. Be sure to measure the length from the very bottom of the frame platform where the pipe originates. Remember that foam rubber offers the most resiliency when it is slightly compressed, so allow an inch or so in your measurement to achieve this resiliency in the finished pipe. It is safer to have too much material as it is a simple matter

to cut excess stock off at the top end. The finished pipe should tend to push away from the frame.

Tapered pipes can be cut to follow the taper of the covering material, or they can be cut rectangularly, using the widest dimension as the basis for the width. The latter method means that more foam rubber will be compressed into the smaller chamber at the lower section of the pipe, offering additional firmness; this gives the occupant greater support at the small of the back. Since the pipe tapers gradually and compresses the foam rubber, bulges do not appear in the finished piece. Many upholsterers endorse this practice because of the additional comfort it provides and the fact that cutting is simplified.

If you decide to taper the foam rubber to coincide with the actual taper of the covering material, it is more economical to reverse the pattern of adjacent pieces when cutting as shown in Fig. 17-30.

Cementing Foam Rubber Pipes

When constructing individual pipes for insertion in fabric pockets, the foam rubber should be rolled to the desired curve and cemented to a backing strip of muslin, so that it will not shift. For the backing strip, cut a piece of muslin to the finished dimensions of the pipe back.

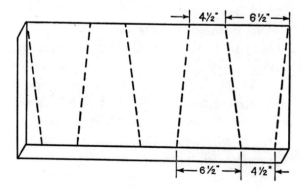

Fig. 17-30. Taper Cutting Layout (Goodyear)

Fig. 17-31. Registering the First Edge (Goodyear)

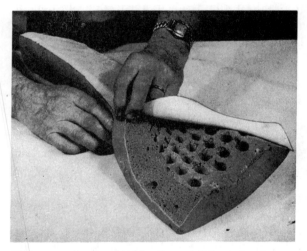

Fig. 17-32. Registering the Second Edge (Goodyear)

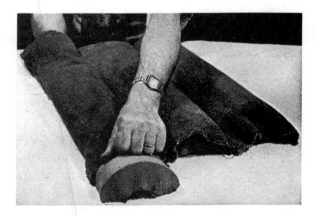

Fig. 17-33. Inserting Pipes (Goodyear)

If the pipe is quite shallow, or if stock of considerable thickness is being used, there may be too much fullness in the center of the longitudinal area of the pipe. This can be reduced by a bevel cut along the bottom edge on each side.

Apply cement to the edge of the foam rubber on each side, and then apply a corresponding amount to the edges of the muslin. Allow the cement to set for a few minutes, and then join one cemented edge of the muslin to an edge of the rubber. See Fig. 17-31.

Position the free edge of the muslin against the other edge of the foam rubber, being sure the edges line up, Fig. 17-32. This pulls the foam rubber to a half-round contour. Hold it in proper position for a few minutes, applying gentle pressure.

Installing Foam Rubber Pipes

If pipe pockets are separate units, foam rubber pipes can be pulled down through the pocket and into place easily, before sewing the finished pipe to the chair. If the entire series of pipes is made from one piece of upholstering fabric, or is joined to the back fabric as a unit, the same procedure of installing the foam rubber pipes can be followed. See Fig. 17-33. When all pipes are in place, the entire unit is sewed and tacked to the chair or sofa.

If the fabric is already in place on the piece, the foam rubber pipes can be inserted by hand. However, if the area is unusually small at the

Fig. 17-34. Metal Inserting Form (Goodyear)

tapered bottom, a regular upholsterer's packing stick or similar blunt-edged tool gives better results. Do not use a sharp-pointed implement. If this type of piping is encountered frequently, the filling operation can be speeded up by making the simple tool illustrated in Fig. 17-34. It can be made of tin, aluminum, galvanized sheet iron, or other light metal. The top section is rounded and the bottom plate is flat, with measurements slightly under actual pipe size to facilitate insertion. To operate, simply enclose the foam rubber pipe within the two sections, insert the unit in the fabric pocket, and withdraw the form. Apply soapstone liberally, so the tool can be easily withdrawn.

Another method of making piped backs is to fabricate a series of foam rubber pipes, install them as a unit, and cover them with fabric, using drawstrings to keep the fabric pulled down.

A more detailed procedure for this method follows:

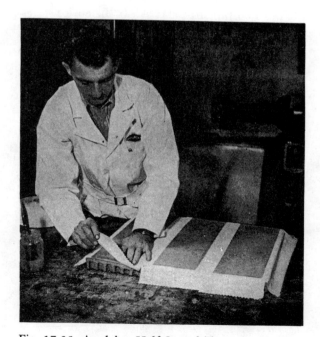

Fig. 17-35. Applying Half-Spread Tapes for Tacking (Goodyear)

1. Cut pipes from foam rubber cored stock as explained earlier. Place them side by side, edges touching, skin side up.
2. Using pre-cemented full-spread tape (1½ or 2 inches wide), tape the sections together. The tapes should extend a couple of inches over the top and bottom for tacking. For the two end pieces, use half-spread tape on the outside edges because these will be tacked to the frame later. See Fig. 17-35.
3. Mark off the pipe divisions on the top and bottom rails of the chair frame.
4. Starting at one side of the frame, tack the tape of the first pipe to the frame edge. Align the foam rubber edge so that it lies flush with the vertical frame edge. Curl the first pipe so that it fits in the area marked off on the top frame rail.
5. Tack the tape joining the first and second pipes to the top rail on the first division line. Do the same at the bottom rail.
6. Work across the frame in this manner until the pipes are completely installed, and finally tack the last outer edge to the frame side.
7. Sew draw cords in the covering fabric where pipes will divide.
8. Anchor the drawstrings and the fabric at the bottom of the frame. Pull the strings up tight over the top and tack in place.
9. Since the fabric is tacked at the bottom rail, it is stretched into position along with the drawstrings and tacked at the top rail.

Buttoning and Tufting

Buttoning (plain, pleated, or tufted) is a relatively simple procedure when working with foam rubber. When buttoning is to be done, soft cored utility stock of #1 or #2 compression should be used. For most applications, the cushion thickness should be at least 1½ inches and not more than 3 inches. The exceptions would be in upholstering large pieces, such as club davenports, where it is entirely practical to use stock as thick as 4½ inches.

Plain Buttoning

For plain buttoning, cut the foam rubber to the desired shape, using actual measurements, plus upholstering allowance and any additional allowance for the desired edge. For an extra firm back, allow an extra ½ inch per button on both the length and the width.

1. Draw the pattern scheme for the location of the buttons onto both the chair platform and the foam rubber.
2. If thick gauge foam rubber is used, a smoother job will result if holes are punched through the foam rubber at the button locations; use a ¾-inch hollow steel punch or ordinary shears.
3. Cement or tape the foam rubber to the chair back.

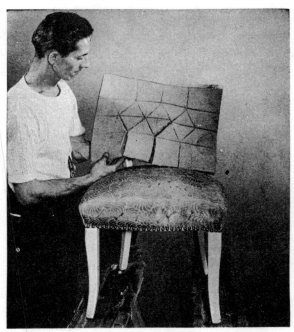

Fig. 17-36. Foam Rubber Slit for Tufted Buttoning
(Goodyear)

4. Covering material is applied in the conventional manner.
5. Install the buttons, starting at the center and working toward the edges. Run a piece of mattress twine through the button; center the button on the length of the twine. Put both ends of twine through the eye of a long straight needle. Pass the needle through the fabric covering and the foam rubber from the front side. Separate the two strands at the back and place a wad of cotton between them. Draw the button into position by tying a square knot behind the cotton wad. The amount of tension applied will determine the depth of the button. The cotton wad prevents the tie from pulling through.

Pleated or Tufted Buttoning

To determine the fabric requirements for pleated or tufted buttoning, begin measuring at the edge of the back. Bring the tape to the bottom of the first hole. Work across the area in this manner to the opposite edge being sure to make sufficient allowances at either end for tacking. In measuring, apply a slight tension to the tape as you draw it from hole to hole, so that the foam rubber assumes a rounded form. Follow the same procedure for vertical measurements.

For pleated or tufted buttoning, the pleats will lie better if the foam rubber is slit in each direction from the hole. Use a sharp knife, single-edged razor blade, or shears, making the slits ½ inch deep or to the point where the cores begin. Cut only along the surface where deep pleats are desired. See Fig. 17-36.

In fashioning pleated tufts, some upholsterers start at the center and work toward each edge while others start at one edge and work across. In either case, each pleat is hand-fashioned as each button is added. See Figs. 17-37 and 17-38. All other operations for pleated or tufted buttons are the same as those described for plain buttoning. A completed chair with pleated back is shown in Fig. 17-39.

Fig.17-37. Position of Buttons and Tufts Marked on Burlap (Goodyear)

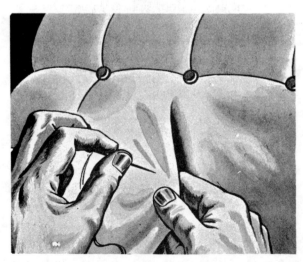

Fig. 17-38. Fashioning a Pleat and Inserting a Button (Dunlop)

Selecting and Applying Covering Materials

A wide range of covering materials can be used over foam rubber; however, those which have a tendency to stretch excessively should be avoided as they will not hold a neat appearance. Covering materials should be drawn down just enough to compress the foam rubber slightly. In cutting the material, make a generous allowance for tacking purposes in order to avoid excessive cover tension that might compress the foam rubber so much that it would reduce its resiliency. Since foam rubber does not pack down, no allowance needs to be made for this when applying the covering. On the other hand, too loose a covering will produce a wrinkled effect.

When to Use Muslin

In using some materials, such as pile, loose weave, slippery fabrics, leather and some plastics, certain precautions need to be followed.

Fig. 17-39. Occasional Chair with Tufted Back (Goodyear)

With most of these materials, it is best to first cover the foam rubber with muslin, duck, or some other inexpensive material. In working with fabrics in the pile group, especially steel-cut velours, the inner cover is a must. The pile is made of individual threads hooked into the base of the cloth. When in direct contact with foam rubber, they rub back and forth as flexing occurs; in time the pile will pull loose from its base. A quick test to determine whether a muslin cover is needed can be made by simply rubbing a piece of foam rubber briskly over the back surface of the cloth in question. If the pile separates from the cloth body, an inner cover should be used.

It is best to cover with muslin first when using: low grade or lightweight leathers (under $3\frac{1}{2}$ ounce); leathers where stretch is definitely noticeable; and plastic coverings without a cloth backing. This will reduce friction and ultimately the tendency to stretch. When using natural leather and cloth-backed plastic, the muslin cover can be omitted; however, the foam rubber used should be one compression firmer than that used with soft fabrics.

Allowing for Air Passage

All leathers and plastics, and even some closely woven fabrics are nonporous to the extent that they do not allow quick passage of air. Some means of allowing for free "breathing" action must be provided. Ventilating grommets can be inserted in the backs of chairs and sofas and the sides of reversible cushions. See Fig. 17-40. The grommet holes permit air

to escape and reenter when the foam rubber is compressed and then released. For nonreversible cushions, an insert of some porous type of upholstery fabric can be used as Fig. 17-41 illustrates. In the case of tight or fixed cushions, the problem does not exist when spring or web construction, or other types of flexible platforms are used because the air can easily escape and reenter. However, when fixed cushions are mounted on a rigid base such as plywood, metal or plastic, and the upholstering material is sealed tightly to the frame, small holes should be drilled through the base at frequent intervals for air passage. The holes do not need to match up with the cores as foam rubber is intercellular.

Fig. 17-40. Grommets in Side of Cushion Provide for Breathing (Goodyear)

Fig. 17-41. Fabric Insert on Non-Reversible Cushion Provides for Breathing (Goodyear)

Foam Rubber Applications

18

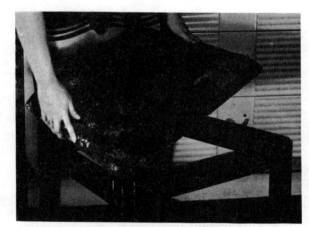

Fig. 18-1. Removing Slip Seat (Natural Rubber)

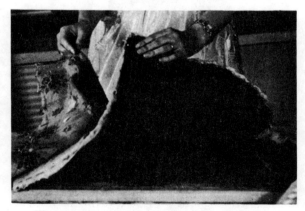

Fig. 18-2. Removing Old Cover and Padding
(Natural Rubber)

Foam rubber is so versatile that its applications are practically unlimited. Some typical applications of foam rubber are illustrated step-by-step in this chapter.

Dining Room Chair Slip Seat

Since slip seats are one of the easiest upholstering jobs to perform they make ideal projects for beginners. The procedure for re-covering a dining room chair slip seat is as follows:

1. Remove the slip seat from the chair and strip off the worn cover and padding, as shown in Figs. 18-1 and 18-2. The seats are usually held by four wood screws counterbored through the seat rails from the bottom or through the corner blocks. They are easily found after the cambric is removed from the bottom of the chair.

2. Lay the frame on cored foam rubber stock two inches thick and trace the shape adding ½ inch allowance on all sides, Fig. 18-3. If the frames are made of plywood, drill holes to permit "breathing."

3. Cut out the foam rubber and bevel all bottom edges as in Fig. 18-4. Dipping shears in water will aid in cutting.

4. Cement tape to all top edges, letting it extend far enough so that it can be easily tacked to bottom of frame. See Fig. 18-5.

5. Tack the tape to the frame, starting first at the centers of all four sides and working toward the corners, Fig. 18-6.

6. Place new covering over seat and tack to bottom of frame. See Fig. 18-7. Tack at centers first and work toward corners

pulling cover uniformly as you tack. Avoid bulkiness as you overlap corners. Remove excess covering material if it is bulky, but be sure to tack firmly. Be certain that tacks are not too long.

7. Replace the re-covered slip seat in the chair, screwing it into position, Fig. 18-8. Tack new cambric to bottom of chair.

Fig. 18-3. Laying Out Shape (Natural Rubber)

Fig. 18-6. Tacking Tape to Bottom of Frame
(Natural Rubber)

Fig. 18-4. Beveling Bottom Edges (Natural Rubber)

Fig. 18-7. Tacking Cover to Frame (Natural Rubber)

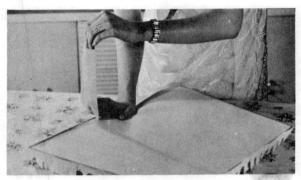

Fig. 18-5. Cementing Tape to Top Edges of Seat
(Natural Rubber)

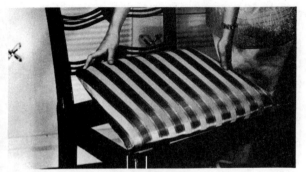

Fig. 18-8. Replacing Slip Seat in Finished Chair
(Natural Rubber)

Kitchen Chair Seat

Re-covering the seats of metal kitchen chairs with foam rubber is another easy upholstery job. The procedure is similar to that just described for slip seats for dining room chairs except that solid slab foam rubber is used and the base is solid plywood. The procedure is as follows:

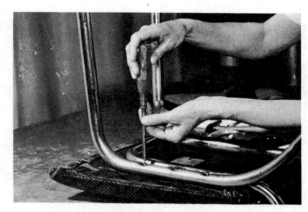

Fig. 18-9. Removing Seat from Kitchen Chair (Goodyear)

Fig. 18-10. Removing Tacks from Covering Material (Goodyear)

Fig. 18-11. Applying Adhesive to Base (Goodyear)

1. Separate seat from chair frame by removing screws from bottom of chair, Fig. 18-9.
2. Remove old covering and padding material using a mallet and ripping tool. If these tools are not available, a screwdriver and hammer can be used as Fig. 18-10 shows.
3. Trace seat design on solid slab foam rubber 1-inch thick. Allow 1/4-inch extra allowance on all sides.
4. Cut out foam rubber, following the tracing, and bevel the bottom edge on all sides.
5. Drill 1/4-inch holes about 2 inches apart all over the seat. Be sure the edges of the holes are smooth.
6. Cement the cushion onto the base with beveled edges toward seat, Fig. 18-11.
7. Place seat on upholstering material, and cut

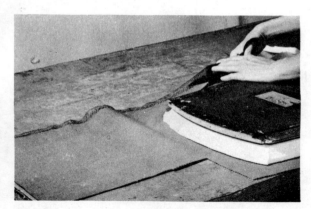

Fig. 18-12. Cutting Upholstering Material (Goodyear)

Fig. 18-13. Folding Excess Material at Corners (Goodyear)

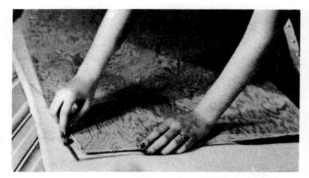

Fig. 18-14. Laying Out Shape on Foam Rubber
(Natural Rubber)

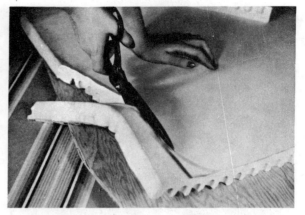

Fig. 18-15. Cutting Top Curvature of Headboard
(Natural Rubber)

out the material allowing at least 2 inches on each side for tacking. See Fig. 18-12.

8. Tack upholstery material in place starting at the center of each side and working toward the corners. Use No. 3 tacks and pull covering material uniformly. Tack corners last, tucking in excess to get a tight fit, as shown in Fig. 18-13.

Padded Headboard

A padded headboard for a bed is an easy upholstering job which will give any bedroom that "decorator look." Begin by cutting ¼- or ⅜-inch plywood to the size and shape of the desired headboard. The covering procedure follows:

1. Make a paper pattern or use the plywood headboard as a pattern. Trace the outline on cored slab foam rubber (of any desired thickness) adding ½-inch allowance on each side. See Fig. 18-14.
2. Cut out foam rubber as shown in Fig. 18-15. Bevel top and sides on under surface.
3. Apply tacking tape on all four sides.
4. Smooth cushioned edges under and tack the tape in place on the headboard. Note Fig. 18-16.
5. Tack covering fabric in place, starting at centers and smoothing material as you work toward the corners, Fig. 18-17.

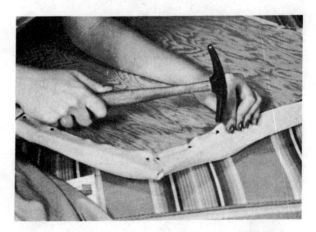

Fig. 18-16. Tacking Tapes at Back (Natural Rubber)

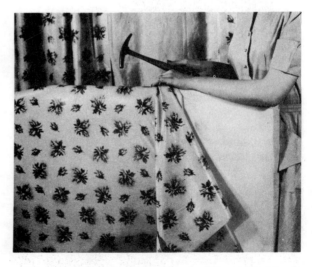

Fig. 18-17. Tacking Fabric Cover (Natural Rubber)

Occasional Chair

The following illustrations show how an old battered occasional chair was restored to better than new condition in appearance and

Fig. 18-18. Occasional Chair before Reupholstering
(U.S. Rubber)

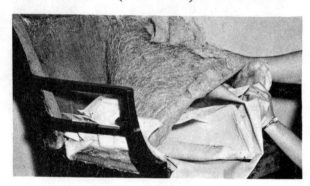

Fig. 18-19. Stripping Chair (U.S. Rubber)

Fig. 18-20. Springs, Burlap, and Webbing Installed
(U.S. Rubber)

comfort using foam rubber and plastic-coated stretch fabric. See Fig. 18-18. The necessary materials included (in addition to equipment such as hammer, tacks, scissors, pencil and paper): 2 pieces of slab foam rubber, 1½ inches thick, 18 inches wide, and 20 inches long; 2 yards of upholstering material; 4 strips of webbing 20 inches long; 4½ yards of tacking tape, 3 inches wide; 5 No-Sag 20-inch springs; 1 piece of reinforced burlap, 20 x 22 inches; and 1 tube of rubber cement. The reupholstering procedure for such a piece is as follows:

1. Strip the old covering and stuffing material, removing everything down to the bare frame, Fig. 18-19.
2. Install five No-Sag springs across the seat.
3. Cover the springs with reinforced burlap.
4. Place four strips of webbing on the back. See Fig. 18-20.
5. Make paper patterns of the seat and back as shown in Fig. 18-21.
6. Using these patterns, lay out the 1½-inch thick solid slab foam rubber, allowing ¼ inch extra on all sides.
7. Cut the foam rubber with scissors, dipping the blades in water to prevent slipping.

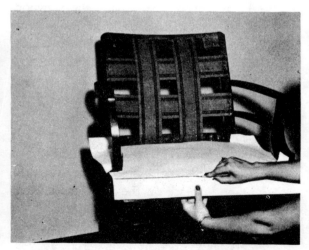

Fig. 18-21. Making Paper Pattern (U.S. Rubber)

Fig. 18-22. Cementing Tacking Tape (U.S. Rubber)

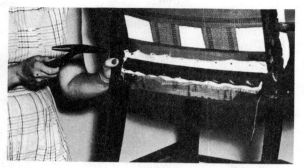

Fig. 18-24. Tacking Back of Seat Cover
(U.S. Rubber)

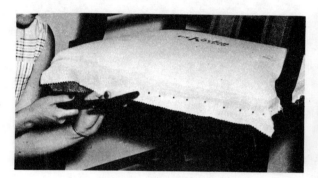

Fig. 18-23. Tacking Seat Cushion in Place
(U.S. Rubber)

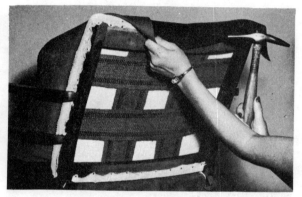

Fig. 18-25. Covering Back (U.S. Rubber)

8. Cement the 3-inch tacking tape along the upper edge of all four sides of seat; half should be on the foam rubber and half free, Fig. 18-22.

9. Place foam rubber on seat and tack in position through tacking tape to secure seat cushion to base of chair. See Fig. 18-23. Follow the same procedure for the back of the chair.

10. Measure depth and width of the chair seat for the covering material. Be sure to allow for covering the sides of the seat and add at least 1 inch for tacking the material to the underside of the chair frame.

11. Cut out covering material, place in position, and tack to bottom of chair frame at the front and sides. Start at center of sides; pulling material taut, work toward corners. The back of the seat is tacked

to the back of the base of the chair seat as shown in Fig. 18-24.

12. Finish with decorative antique brass tacks.

13. Measure back for covering material, cut it out, and position it.

14. Tack covering to the back, base of chair, and sides of back starting at centers and working toward corners. See Fig. 18-25. Make neat, folded corners. Folds should always be toward the outer edges so they will not catch dust or dirt when dusted, Fig. 18-26.

15. Measure and cut material for outside cover of the back.

16. Invert chair and tack back cover in place using decorative tacks on top and sides. Bottom of back cover is tacked to underneath side of chair base. Fold material under at top and sides before tacking.

Tack material at center of base and top, and work across top from center to top corners and then down the sides toward the base, Fig. 18-27.

17. Tack a piece of cambric or other cloth to the bottom of the chair to catch any

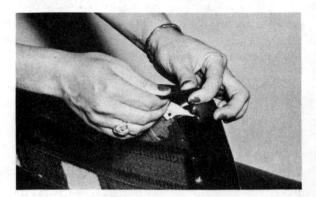

Fig. 18-26. Making Corners (U.S. Rubber)

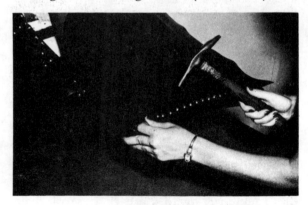

Fig. 18-27. Tacking Back Cover (U.S. Rubber)

Fig. 18-28. Covering Bottom of Chair (U.S. Rubber)

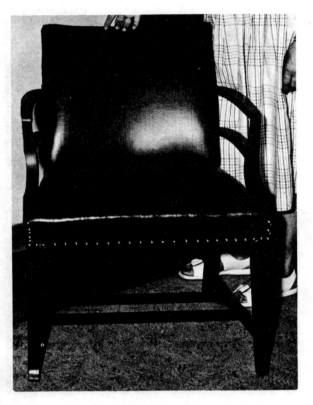

Fig. 18-29. The Reupholstered Occasional Chair (U.S. Rubber)

dust and give the chair a professional look, Fig. 18-28. Fig. 18-29 pictures the finished product.

Reversible Cushion

Reversible cushions for living room sofas or easy chairs can be easily converted to foam rubber if the spring cushion units are damaged. The change may also be desirable just to make them more comfortable. If the covering material of the cushion case is in good condition, the procedure is as follows:

1. Open the rear edge of the cushion cover by carefully cutting the stitches at the welt line with a razor blade or scissors. Remove all of the old padding material and springs.

2. Measure the width, length, and thickness of the cushion case from welt to welt. See

Fig. 18-30. Measuring Cushion Case (Goodyear)

Fig. 18-31. Checking Molded Cushion Unit
(Goodyear)

Fig. 18-32. Sewing Cushion End Held by Skewers
(Goodyear)

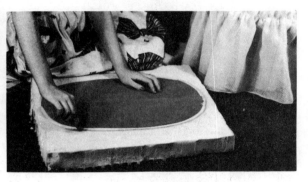

Fig. 18-33. Laying Out Foam Rubber
(Natural Rubber)

Fig. 18-34. Slipping Pad into Cover
(Natural Rubber)

Fig. 18-30. Purchase a reversible molded foam rubber cushion unit ¾ inch or 1 inch longer and wider than the cover measurements to insure a snug fit. Make no extra allowance on the thickness. Note Fig. 18-31.

3. Squeeze the foam rubber cushion unit and insert it into the cushion case.

4. Using upholsterers' pins (skewers) to hold the open end in place, restitch the end, passing the thread under the welt with a regular or curved upholstering needle as shown in Fig. 18-32. A curved needle makes the job easier.

Bassinet Pad

For the brand new member of the family, a latex foam mattress is the last word in comfort. It is simple to make and easy to clean — just wash it. Follow these instructions:

1. Cut a paper pattern to size and trace it on the foam rubber making ½-inch over-allowance as shown in Fig. 18-33.

2. Cut foam rubber along traced line, taking care to keep edge square. Dipping blades of shears in water aids cutting.

3. Cement tacking tape flat against all sides.

4. Slip the pad into a washable or waterproof cover and you have a finished mattress fit for a prince or princess, Fig. 18-34.

Living Room Chair

The wing chair pictured in Fig. 18-35 was redesigned to modernize it, and reupholstered with foam rubber to make it more comfortable. The frame was in good condition, but the springs were not. It was decided to change the seat from platform construction to helical springs. See Fig. 18-36. Such a seat is made as follows:

1. Tack heavy wrapping paper in place on seat for use as a pattern. Invert chair to mark pattern along inside dimensions of frame. Remove paper and cut out pattern.

2. On this pattern, mark another line 2½ inches in from all sides. Shape upholsterers' border wire, ⅛ inch in diameter, to match this penciled line.

3. Place a piece of 12-ounce duck over wire frame and cut, allowing a 5-inch overlap on all sides.

4. Double stitch the duck around the wire, remembering 5-inch overlap. Punch holes through ducking between wire frame and double stitching. The holes should be 3½ to 4 inches apart.

5. Insert 14-gauge helical springs in these holes.

6. For anchoring the springs to the frame use 1-inch long metal tabs with ⅛-inch holes located 3/16 of an inch from each end. Tack these to the frame, with one hole flush against the inside edge. Space the tabs 3½ to 4 inches apart, matching holes punched

Fig. 18-35. Old Styled Modified Wing Chair (Goodyear)

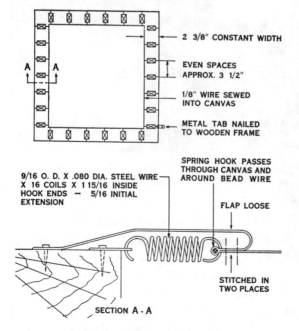

Fig. 18-36. Layout for Helical Spring Flexible Platform (Goodyear)

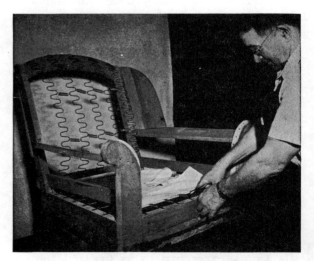

Fig. 18-37. Stretching Helical Springs to Metal Tabs on New Platform Rails (Goodyear)

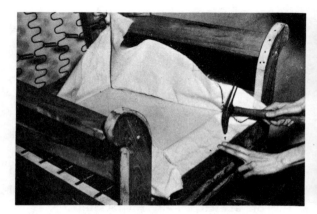

Fig. 18-38. Tacking Ducking to Frame (Goodyear)

Fig. 18-39. Tacking Muslin to Frame (Goodyear)

in duck, for a straight pull on the springs and wire frame.

7. Hook springs to metal tabs on all sides of chair frame. See Fig. 18-37.

8. Tack overlapped ducking loosely to frame to allow for spring sag when body weight is applied, Fig. 18-38.

9. Across the back, equally space five zigzag springs and fasten at top and bottom by clips. To figure the proper crown to be made in back add depth of cushion and thickness of foam rubber cored stock to be used. Arch springs to allow for this measurement between front rail and crown or arch of springs.

10. Clip helical springs between zigzag springs to hold them in place.

11. Place a thin layer of cotton batting over seat suspension.

12. Cut muslin and tack to outside of seat on all four sides as shown in Fig. 18-39. Trim off excess muslin.

Finishing the Chair

The following procedures describe the remainder of the reupholstery job.

1. Make a deck roll by cutting a ¾-inch piece of slab foam rubber stock 1½ inches wide. Cut a second piece of slab stock 2½

Fig. 18-40. Tacking Covering of Seat Platform over Foam Rubber Deck Roll (Goodyear)

inches wide. Place this on top of the first piece, flush at the front. Cover both pieces with a thin layer of cotton.

2. Cut a piece of chair covering material as wide as the width of the chair and sufficiently long to cover the deck roll of foam rubber. Stitch this piece of covering material to a piece of muslin covering that will cover the seat.

3. Tack muslin covering over seat, and pull material covering over deck roll with a slight tension; tack it into place on front frame rail as shown in Fig. 18-40.

4. Tack burlap to inside of arm rest frame. Fill out frame depth with a filler material such as moss or tow, and tack burlap on

outside of arm rest frame to hold filler in place, Fig. 18-41.

5. Do the same for the other arm.

6. Make arm and wing patterns. Tack heavy paper to frame and mark contour of arm and wing with heavy pencil for cutting. See Figs. 18-42 and 18-43.

7. Trace patterns on ¾- or 1-inch thick slab stock and cut them out. Cut material for wings about an inch narrower than pattern at back to allow room for tacking back cushion covering material.

8. Cement muslin tacking tape, about 5 inches wide, to foam rubber leaving half of tape edge loose for tacking.

9. Tack material through tacking tape to arms and wings. See Figs. 18-44 and 18-45.

10. Cement the foam rubber flush against inside of wing frame by applying rubber

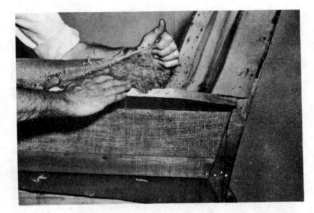

Fig. 18-41. Stuffing Filler on Arm Rest (Goodyear)

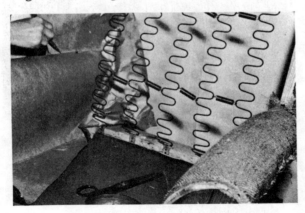

Fig. 18-42. Making Pattern for Arm (Goodyear)

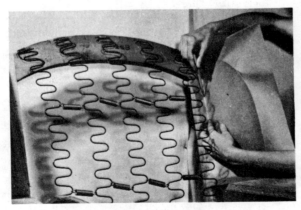

Fig. 18-43. Making Pattern for Wing (Goodyear)

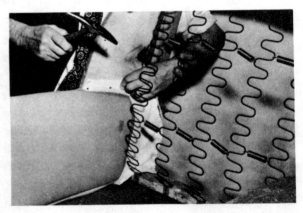

Fig. 18-44. Tacking Back of Arm through Tape (Goodyear)

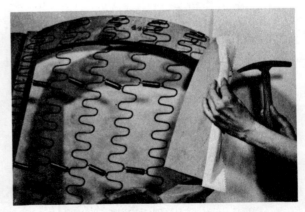

Fig. 18-45. Tacking Wing through Tacking Tape (Goodyear)

adhesive to the surfaces of the frame and the foam rubber. See Fig. 18-46.

11. Cover arms and wings with covering material. The same patterns used for cutting the foam rubber may be used for cutting the covering material by allowing 2 or 3 inches on each side for tacking.

12. Place burlap over back springs and cover with cotton padding as shown in Fig. 18-47.

13. Tack paper into place on the back and mark a pattern. See Fig. 18-48.

14. Cut foam rubber to shape and apply tape as you did for the arms and wings.

15. Tack into place at top, bottom, and wing frames.

16. Cover the other parts of the chair with covering material in the following se-

Fig. 18-48. Making Paper Pattern for Back (Goodyear)

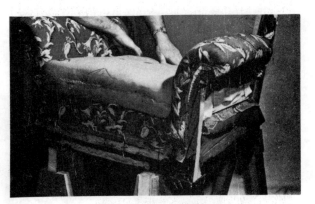
Fig. 18-49. Checking Molded Cushion Unit (Goodyear)

Fig. 18-46. Cementing Wing Frame (Goodyear)

Fig. 18-50. Finished Modernized Wing Chair (Goodyear)

Fig. 18-47. Placing Cotton over Burlap (Goodyear)

quence: front of chair, a welt across top of this piece makes it more attractive; outside covers of wings; outside covers of arms; back cover; and cambric on the bottom of chair.

17. Select a 5½-inch crown molded cushion, about 1 inch larger in length and width than the seat of the chair, Fig. 18-49. Cover the cushion with covering material.

18. Refinish legs if necessary, and you have a "new" chair, Fig. 18-50.

Miscellaneous Applications

The following illustrations show some of the many varied applications of foam rubber. It is used in the automobile industry for upholstering seats and backs; first it was employed in combination with springs and later without any springs. See Figs. 18-51 and 18-52. Foam rubber is also used in automobiles as a safety measure in padded dashboards, sun visors, arm rests, and side panels. Even bus seats are made from molded one-piece units.

The aircraft industry uses foam rubber because of its light weight and high comfort qualities. It is used in airplane seats, footrests, and as padding on fuselage walls and compartments for safety.

In the bedding industry, foam rubber is used in mattresses for homes and hospitals, as pictured in Fig. 18-53. Cored foam rubber slab stock at least 3 inches thick is ideally suited for children's cribs.

Foam rubber is widely used in the manufacture and reupholstering of office furniture.

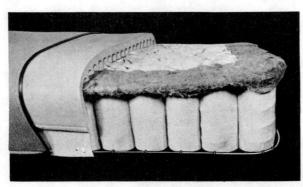

Fig. 18-51. Automobile Seat with Foam Rubber over Springs (U.S. Rubber)

Fig. 18-53. Hospital Bed (U.S. Rubber)

Fig. 18-52. All-Foam-Rubber Automobile Seats and Backs (U.S. Rubber)

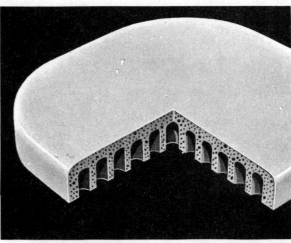

Fig. 18-54. Office Chair Molded Cushion Unit (Dunlop)

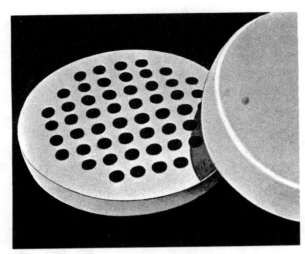

Fig. 18-55. Molded Stool Cushion Unit (Dunlop)

Fig. 18-56. Wedge-Shaped Bolster (Natural Rubber)

Fig. 18-57. Outdoor Chaise Lounge (Goodyear)

Molded and shaped one-piece units are available for executive chairs, with solid bases and well-crowned units for upholstery cover protection. Thin, padded, posture-shaped backs and molded cushion units are made for stenographic chairs. Individual molded foam rubber cushion units are also manufactured for general office chairs. See Fig. 18-54.

In combination with individual cushions, wedged-shaped units can be arranged as a floor chaise lounge or a hassock for the recreation room, family room, or living room.

Molded foam rubber units or slab stock can be used for such applications as stools, wedge-shaped bolsters, piano benches, outdoor furniture, and bathinette pads. Note Figs. 18-55 through 18-57. The ease with which foam rubber units may be attached to frames of any design makes it particularly suited for upholstering modern metal or wood furniture.

Manufacture of Foam Rubber 19

Foam rubber is manufactured from *latex*, rubber in its original fluid form. After chemicals have been added to the latex for catalytic and preservative actions, it is put into a mixing machine. As millions of tiny interconnecting air cells are whipped into it, it becomes a fluffy froth-like foam. See Fig. 19-1. The latex foam is then poured into a two-piece mold and vulcanized into the permanent shape of the mold. The process is similar to that employed in the home in baking a cake where the ingredients are whipped up in a mixer, the batter is poured into a pan, and the cake is placed in the oven to bake. The foam rubber product even feels and looks like a soft angel food cake. A detailed description of the manufacturing process follows.

Fig. 19-1. Magnified View of Foam Rubber Showing Interconnecting Cells (U.S. Rubber)

Collecting Liquid Latex

Latex is collected from rubber trees grown on plantations in Southeast Asia (in Malaya and Sumatra) and in Liberia in Africa. Natural liquid latex is the pure milk of the rubber tree. It flows between the bark and the main core or trunk of the tree. Since it is not the sap of the tree, the bark can be cut year after year and the milk drained from the tree as shown in Fig. 19-2. Rubber latex is also made synthetically; the synthetic product has some advantages over the natural product. Rubber laboratories are endeavoring to blend both natural and synthetic rubber into compounds that will be even superior to the natural rubber latex.

At the present time, the natural liquid latex is collected in cups drop by drop, transferred to milk cans and transported to central collection stations similar to the one pictured in Fig. 19-3. Here it is mixed with a preservative and concentrated. It is shipped in its creamy liquid condition in huge tanks by rail and boat to latex manufacturers in the United States. At the latex factories it is stored in large tanks under controlled conditions that keep the liquid latex uniform until used in production.

Mixing and Foaming

The first step in processing foam rubber is the mixing of the latex in large agitating tanks with ingredients such as sulphur and other powders which are ground in ball mills, Fig. 19-4. The latex is also aged in these tanks.

The next procedure is the foaming or frothing process which is performed by giant mixers resembling egg beaters. See Fig. 19-5. During this foaming process the latex is whipped to a creamy froth while the texture and firmness of

Fig. 19-2. Tapping Rubber Tree on Liberian Plantation (Firestone)

Fig. 19-4. Agitating Tanks (Dunlop)

Fig. 19-3. Central Collection Station for Latex (Goodyear)

Fig. 19-5. Battery of 8,000-Gallon Latex Mixers (Dunlop)

the finished material are controlled. More whipping injects more air bubbles and causes the foam rubber to be lighter and softer. A cubic inch of solid slab foam rubber contains over a quarter of a million tiny air cells making it about 85 percent air. Cored foam rubber is from 90 to 95 percent air. The foaming process may also be performed by incorporating in the latex a material which causes it to foam.

Molding

When the foamed compound has reached the right consistency, the frothy mixture is poured into metal molds. See Fig. 19-6. The metal molds consist of two pieces as Fig. 19-7 shows. The bottom piece, called the pan, is the receiving cavity for the liquid foam and is engineered to the exact size and shape of the designed foam rubber unit. The top piece, called the top plate, is a flat plate to which many core pins are attached. This top plate is used when molding cored units; when used without the core pins, solid units can be manufactured. When the top plate is placed over the pan, the core pins extend down into the pan.

After the liquid foam is poured into the molds, the molds enter giant ovens for curing or "baking" under controlled heat and pressure. When the curing process is completed, the foam rubber units are pulled or stripped from the molds. See Fig. 19-8. The "flash" is trimmed from the molded units; this is any excess that has escaped from the mold between the pan and the top plate. The piece is then sent by conveyor belt to a washing machine to remove all impurities, and conveyed by belt to electronic drying ovens, Fig. 19-9.

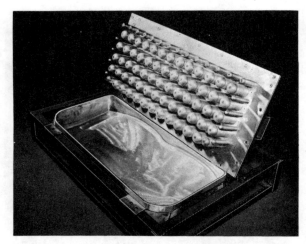

Fig. 19-7. A Typical Mold for a Two-Passenger Transportation Seat Unit (U.S. Rubber)

Fig. 19-6. Pouring Latex into Multiple Mold (Goodyear)

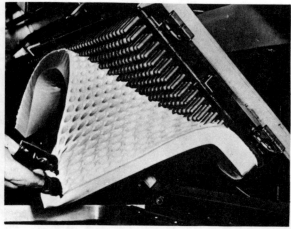

Fig. 19-8. Stripping Cured Mattress from Mold (Dunlop)

Fig. 19-9. Cured Mattress Emerging from
Washing Machine (Dunlop)

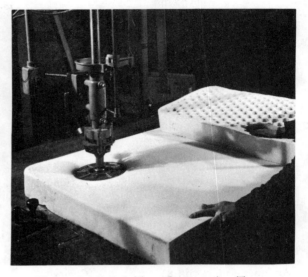

Fig. 19-10. Bench Type Compression Tester
(Goodyear)

Finishing Processes

As the units emerge from the dryer, they are
inspected for any visible defects. They then go
onto an inspection conveyor where any remaining pieces of flash are snipped off with shears.
Finally the units are again conveyed by belt
to machines which automatically test each
for density or compression, as in Fig. 19-10.

The foam rubber manufacturing industry is
highly mechanized, utilizing many electronic
controls. Molds and finished units are moved
by electronically controlled conveyor belts not
only from operation to operation, but from one
floor to another as shown in Fig. 19-11. Automatic conveyor belts are also used extensively
in the shipping departments for handling finished products to package and weigh them,
and for conveying finished packages to loading
platforms or warehouses.

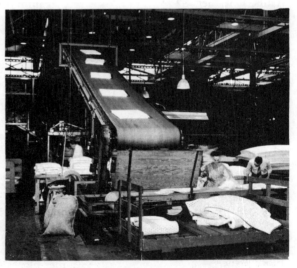

Fig. 19-11. Foam Rubber Units Conveyed by
Belt from Floor to Floor (Goodyear)

Index